More Bang for Your Buck

More Bang
for Your Buck

Peter Heegaard

foreword by
Lori Sturdevant

For
Joe & Mary
Best wishes!
Ph
10/8/11

NODIN PRESS

The author wishes to acknowledge the support of the Urban Adventure Funds at the Greater Twin Cities United Way and the Minneapolis Foundation. Royalties received by the author that exceed expenses will be donated to non-profit organizations featured in this book.

Design: John Toren

ISBN: 978-1-935666-34-9

Cover photos:
mechanic—©Michaeljung / Dreamstime
construction workers—©Jeffbanke/Dreamstime
doctor and patient—©Rmarmion/Dreamstime
classroom—©Brailean/Dreamstime

Nodin Press
530 N Third Street
Suite 120
Minneapolis, MN
55401

For Susan & Gary, Kip & Lucy, and Kate & Rick

Contents

══════ Section One ══════

Applying Return-on-investment Analysis to Well-established, Not-for-profit, Community-based Organizations

Part I

Improving taxpayer returns in education, community development, hunger abatement, corrections and welfare dependence

Part II

Creative approaches to raising the productivity of our investments in housing affordable to families of all ages

Part III

Workforce training organizations that can reduce social service costs and also raise tax revenues

95 / Project for Pride in Living: Health care training partnering academics at a community college with soft and hard skill training at a local hospital

99 / Twin Cities Rise: Market driven training techniques for unemployed adults of color for jobs paying a living wage of at least $25,000

Section Two

Applying Cost/benefit Analysis to Programs That Have Been Replicated Nationally

105 / The Benefits of High Quality Early Childhood Education
Studies indicate that as many as 50% of our children are not fully prepared for kindergarten. This results in lower graduation rates, higher crime rates, fewer working adults and significant added future expense for taxpayers.

117 / Improving High-School Graduation Rates with the Quantum Opportunities Program
After school boost-up education programs involving community service and appropriate motivation can significantly improve high-school graduation rates.

120 / Curing Child Abuse and Neglect with Targeted Home Visitation Programs
When a trained public health nurse meets with a family where child abuse or neglect is observed the payoff for the child, family and community is very large.

123 / Mortgage Foreclosure Prevention Programs Can Be Highly Cost-Effective
Low cost counseling programs when homeowners are defaulting on their mortgage provide enormous savings for families, neighborhoods and all levels of government.

═══ Section Three ═══

The Art of Changing & Improving Public Policy

═══ Section Four ═══

The Application of ROI Analysis by Nationally Acclaimed Research Institutes

Across the USA a number of think tanks have been funded by government and the philanthropic community dedicated to identifying public policy options that improve the economic return on taxpayer dollars. This section highlights several of these organizations and the public policy issues researched.

Foreword

Americans have long held that creating an environment that enables and empowers citizens to be self-sufficient is an essential role of government. Taxpayers have invested heavily in public policy initiatives that support that belief—with decidedly mixed results. The thesis of "More Bang for Your Buck" is that those results would improve if a number of tools that are standard measures of performance in industry were applied to public and not-for-profit anti-poverty programs. Cost/benefit analysis of those programs can determine their return on investment, identify best practices, and guide the formation of effective public policy.

Author Peter Heegaard, a founder and former Managing Principal of Lowry Hill, an investment advisory subsidiary of Wells Fargo Corporation, has spent more than eight years researching how to apply cost/benefit analysis and return-on-investment calculations to selected not-for-profit organizations and public policy initiatives. He has good news to report: A number of the programs he analyzed are successful enough to more than pay for themselves over a relatively short time frame. He shares his analysis of those programs in a format devoid of complex formulas and calculations and therefore understandable to the average reader.

Heegaard applies his analysis to a variety of programs, including those dedicated to preparing young children for school, reducing child abuse and neglect, improving high-school graduation rates, increasing the number of high school graduates going to college, teaching prospective entrepreneurs how to successfully launch a viable neighborhood business, reducing hunger, lowering the rate of recidivism in correctional facilities for young men and giving welfare recipients incentives to work their way to self-sufficiency. Special emphasis is given to creative new approaches to raising the productivity of investments in housing for low-income families, and to mortgage foreclosure prevention. Also included is a special section that reviews job skills training programs that serve individuals with varying developmental capacities.

One section describes a case study of citizens partnering with government to implement computerized data collection systems that permit cost/benefit analyses of publicly funded workforce development programs. The case study demonstrates how, in a period of scarce public resources, emphasis can be placed where the payoff to the taxpayer is known to be greatest. The effort took five years and involved partnerships with five workforce training organizations, two leading regional philanthropic organizations (Greater Twin Cities United Way and Minneapolis Community Foundation), the state of Minnesota's Department of Employment and Economic Development, a leading workforce development consultant and several interested citizens. The result is a database that permits return on investment calculations to be made, thereby demonstrating the benefits and savings job skill training programs can produce.

More Bang issues a call for a new kind of record-keeping by organizations attempting to lift people out of poverty. Much remains to be accomplished in improving the accounting systems that permit one to determine the value added by these organizations and public programs. However, by making conservative assumptions where data may not be complete, reasonable conclusions can be drawn about the time needed for programs to reach their break-even point and thereafter earn a reasonable rate of return for their investors. This book makes clear in each case it examines which data are factual and which are assumed.

Included in the book are presentations by leading research organizations that have undertaken in-depth studies of efforts to tackle poverty. Among them are research projects contracted for by state government that have been helpful in allocating government resources where the payoff is greatest. Finally, *More Bang for Your Buck* offers recommendations for taxpayers, public officials, philanthropic organizations and non-profit managers seeking to use cost/benefit analysis and return-on-investment metrics to more effectively promote the public good.

– Lori Sturdevant
Editorial Writer/Columnist
Minneapolis Star Tribune

Acknowledgements

The initial impetus for this book came from viewing workforce development programs which were a part of the curriculum of the urban education experiential learning program I launched in 1998 after retiring from Lowry Hill, an investment advisory subsidiary of Wells Fargo (formerly Norwest Corporation). "Urban Adventure" as it is called has a curriculum that demonstrates how healthy communities can have a positive impact on business profitability as well as how businesses can help sustain strong economically viable communities. I am indebted to my long term friend and business associate Tom Dolan for helping me structure this program and get it launched. Shortly after I retired I met Steve Rothchild, a retired General Mills senior executive who founded Twin Cities Rise, a recent new entrant to job skill training programs, and who was applying the concept of "return on investment" to his program. Rothchild commissioned professor Raymond Robertson of Macalester College to begin the process of showing how an investment in well managed workforce training programs could generate a positive economic return to the community. This was in the early 2000s. About this same time I became familiar with the pioneering work of the Amos Wilder Foundation of St Paul, Minnesota. Wilder had gained a solid reputation for doing contract research for selective non-profits who wanted to measure the general effectiveness and economic benefit of their work. Other than the work by Wilder little had been done locally in this field since the mid 1990s when the then existing Minnesota State Planning Agency made some initial forays into workforce cost/benefit analysis.

Much of the early credit for this book must go to Steve Rothchild of Twin Cities Rise and the other CEOs of leading workforce training programs who took considerable time and effort to assemble the data that related to the costs and benefits of their programs. These included Jane Samargia of HIRED, Louis King of Summit Academy OIC, Michael

Wirth Davis of Goodwill Easter Seals, Steve Cramer of Project for Pride in Living, Deborah Atterberry of Resource Inc. and Rothchild's successors Mike Bingham and Arthur Berman.

About the same time as it became clear that a creditable case could be made for demonstrating the favorable economic payoff from well-managed job skill training programs other applications surfaced. Art Rolnick, Chief Economist for the Ninth Federal Reserve District at that time, had initiated a remarkable study in concert with his colleague Rob Grunewald that detailed the significant economic contribution of high quality early childhood (pre-kindergarten) education programs. They went through an exhaustive process of quantifying the benefits from a forty year longitudinal study performed on a high quality pre-school program in Yipsilanti, Michigan in 1962.

These successful applications of cost/benefit analysis provided the motivation for me to explore still other areas where the data wasn't always complete but where reasonable assumptions could be made as to possible outcomes. With some of the studies local initiatives could draw upon national research which was helpful in improving the credibility of the analysis. In other cases only a non-profit organization's annual reports and other published materials were available. The work of Rich Cowles and the St Paul based Charities Review Council was helpful in structuring the format of the non-profit reviews. Louise Brown, former Research Director for Family & Children's Service of Minnesota was extremely helpful in providing cost/benefit analysis studies for programs that work to help families move out of poverty and achieve self-sufficiency.

In addition to those mentioned earlier I am indebted to the following non-profit CEOs who also participated in these cost/benefit studies: Trixie Ann Golberg, Life Track Resources; Gloria Perez, Jeremiah Program; Jim McCorkell, Admission Possible; Tracy Fishman and Bonnie Esposito, AcountAbility Minnesota; Jeff Washburn, City of Lakes Land Trust; Susan Haigh, Minnesota Habitat for Humanity; Robert Zeaske, Second Harvest Heartland; Mike Temali, Neighborhood Development Center; Bill and Gail Roddy, Osirus Program and Paul Fate and Joe Errigo of Common Bond Communities.

There were a number of individuals who came together to complete the public policy work impacting the Minnesota Department of Employment & Economic Development outlined in Section Three of this book. Mayor RT Rybak and CPED Director Mike Christenson of the City of Minneapolis were early supporters of applying ROI analysis to the city's workforce programs headed initially by Mike Brinda and later by Deb Bahr-Helgen. Libby Starling currently serving with the Greater Twin Cities Metropolitan Council was the first to indicate that data bases were in place at DEED from which a system of performance measurement could be developed. Deb Serum of DEED was instrumental in integrating and linking the data bases of these workforce training programs with the state systems.

Luke Weisberg of LukeWorks,LLC became the consultant and project manager for the entire effort with DEED. Paul Anton of the Wilder Foundation played a key role in the initial design of the project insuring that final outcomes would be in a format appropriate for creditable ROI analysis as was Chip Wells of Hennepin County. The Greater Twin Cities United Way and The Northstar Fund of the Minneapolis Foundation provided the funding for this multi year project involving the Minnesota Department of Employment & Economic Development. At the Greater Twin Cities United Way the leadership team included Marcia Fink, Devon Meade and Brian Paulson. At the Minneapolis Foundation Eric Anderson coordinated the work of the North Star Fund whose board I served on along with Donald Brown, Libby Carrier Doran and Bridget Hust.

With respect to the complex process of trying to determine what the true savings are from working ones way off of welfare I am indebted to several individuals. Our accountant Amanda Giliotti was the first to open my eyes to the wide range of credits and benefits available to low income families and individuals in Minnesota. Mark Kieczweski of the Minnesota Department of Human Services and State Demographer Tom Gillaspy each lent their expertise in pointing out both the benefits and need for ongoing refinement of the state's complex system of cash and non-cash benefits to low income individuals attempting to work their way off of welfare.

Others who took time to read through the transcript and make constructive suggestions include educator and former mayor of St Paul George Latimer, Ninth Federal Reserve Board economist Arthur Rolnick, Paul Anton formerly of the Wilder Foundation, former member of the governor's workforce council Luke Weisberg, Dane Smith of Growth & Justice, and Raymond Robertson, Professor of Economics at Macalester College. In addition, local public affairs consultant Chuck Slocum was especially helpful in pulling together a distribution plan for the book. I am especially indebted to Lori Sturdevant, my editor, whose lifelong devotion to efforts that enhance public dialogue and public policy are well known both locally and nationally. Twin City publishing consultant John Toren managed the design and production of the book. Finally my wife and life partner Anne Mintener Heegaard has shared many of these adventures with me and is responsible more than anyone else for introducing me to the incredibly stimulating world of community based non-profit organizations.

Introduction

Wiser spending—more bang for our bucks—has become a national imperative since America slid into the Great Recession in 2008. In the United States today our financial resources are becoming more limited at the same time that the challenges to our economic and social progress increase. Yet new thinking is emerging about techniques to improve the process of resource allocation.The studies included in this book demonstrate that we can greatly improve the returns on the taxes we pay with the added prospect of actually reducing some key expense areas in the years ahead. This is particularly true with respect to reducing unemployment, moving families from poverty to self-sufficiency and reducing social service and criminal justice system expenses.There are hopeful signs emerging that we now know what works. The question is whether we have the willpower and commitment to sacrifice what is required to bring about constructive change.

Enough examples of high payoff civic investments now exist to make a very strong case that the art of giving or philanthropic investing, including government budget decision making, can create new solutions to age old problems while at the same time improving the returns on our taxable income. Often as citizens we question whether our tax dollars are being spent wisely. Federal, state and county budgets are complex and are usually not in a format that renders it easy to match spending with outcomes. Are we as citizens really getting the return on our investment in government that we deserve? Elected officials ask the same question in structuring government budgets. "How do we know that we are putting taxpayer dollars where they will do the most good," they ask themselves.

Measure twice and cut once is the age old rule of carpentry. The same rule can be applied to our public investments where in many cases we either don't measure at all or if we do the result is not in a format that can often be communicated in an understandable way to the average taxpaying citizen. This book should interest taxpayers, elected officials, government department heads, non-profit managers, foundation executives and philanthropic investors who wish to make the type of creative investments in their communities that bring constructive change and serve people in the most helpful and cost effective way.

As an interested citizen I have attempted to draw upon a few of the analytical techniques applied with for profit company analysis from nearly forty years in the financial services industry to well managed non-profit organizations. My approach is less complex than the techniques used in the heavily documented studies performed by some of the leading national research organizations which are highlighted later in the book. Nevertheless, I believe the assumptions to be conservative, the methodology applied to be accurate and the results to clearly demonstrate that cost/benefit calculations can be applied to many public and private organizations demonstrating their significant economic contribution to the community. In addition where government funding supports these organizations as part of broader public policy objectives the result can be more efficient and effective use of taxpayer dollars.

Major non-profit and public policy sectors covered in the text include initiatives in the fields of workforce development, affordable housing, early childhood education, K-12 education, criminal justice system, delaying or avoiding nursing home care, moving families from welfare dependence to self-sufficiency, community economic development and hunger abatement.

Elected officials and major foundations do not enjoy the luxury we have as individuals of letting personal experience and preference influence their financial decisions. Their job is to allocate dollars where the greatest benefit can be obtained. Given the public scrutiny and political pressures that exist today the job of allocating public resources effectively is difficult to say the least. What further complicates the process is the lack of standard performance measures that minimize political skirmishing and permit creditable evaluation of the results achieved. In addition, the budgets of many of our major governmental institutions do not include funding for program evaluation.

As individuals we ask the same question when trying to respond to the multitude of requests we get for contributions to this cause or that. How much should we set aside for the church or the United Way, Red Cross, Cancer Research Fund, the local food shelf or the long list of charities that seek our support. Often our giving decisions relate to an event that sensitized us to a particular cause be it medically related or from some random experience that put us into contact with someone who can gain self sufficiency and a new life from the support of a non-profit organization.

Most business managers and investors in ongoing commercial enterprises generally begin by asking the question, "How many dollars of sales am I getting out of my business each year for each dollar invested?" They then ask, "How many dollars of earnings do I receive for every dollar of sales?" These two ratios are at the heart of the financial analysis that influences much of the free world's economy. Finally the investor or business manager puts these two ratios together and calculates the net earnings generated on each dollar of capital invested in the business or the return on investment (ROI). That final ratio answers the often asked question, "What is the return on investment (the ROI) for this business?" With these calculations businesses can be compared with respect to their financial attractiveness within industries as well as across the entire spectrum of the world wide economy. This analysis is based on a financial accounting system that has existed for hundreds of years and is international in scope. It is the language of commerce and it permits a disciplined approach to evaluating the value derived from the allocation of scarce resources.

Nothing fully comparable has evolved to assist government or philanthropic investors. We do have cost accounting systems that track the cost of different spending decisions. We also have financial control systems that insure that money is not lost to theft or neglect but nothing quite comparable to the calculation of "Return on Investment" that exists in the world of commerce and finance. Some new tools and methodologies are beginning to emerge, however, that suggest a significant start is being made in upgrading the financial analysis of programs that seek to improve the economic and social well being of our citizens. Some programs are privately funded, others sponsored by government and still others in the format of public-private partnerships. We will explore some of these new techniques in the pages that follow.

Leading think tanks which are performing extensive research on the art of evaluating social investment returns look at three basic methodologies for evaluating the benefits from changes in economic status of social service recipients. One measure which will be used in the studies which follow looks at the economic return to taxpayers as determined by reductions in public assistance and gains in federal and state tax receipts. Another measure reviews changes in net disposable income for individual service beneficiaries. In other words asking the question, have we really improved the economic status of this individual or family. A final measure observes the total impact of social service programs and the individuals involved on the economy as a whole.

ROI is but one tool to be used in program analysis. To be creditable it must be used in a professional management setting where data about the individuals affected can be collected. The data collection process must be thorough and objective with respect to both program costs and program benefits. That is why considerable space is devoted to management experience, organizational expertise and professional governance systems in the program studies which follow.

More Bang for Your Buck

Section One

Calculating the return on investment of well-established, community-based non-profit organizations is akin to the assessments I often made of for-profit companies as an investment executive. But as this section illustrates with 16 examples, grouped into three parts, there are key differences as well. My non-profit ROI takes into account the needs that are satisfied by the services the organizations provide, the strength of their management, testimonials from clients who benefited from their services, and the financial results as measured by their impact on the community as well as on taxpayers.

In each of the 16 case studies that follow, my analysis is based upon annual reports and other publications of the non-profit organizations, management interviews and personal observations of how well these organizations perform against their stated objectives. The calculations used to compute their return on investment require a number of assumptions to be made about the cost and economic benefit of their programs. In certain cases data is derived from studies completed by governmental and well-established national and local research organizations. The assumptions are thought to be conservative. But clearly, there is room for debate about the nature of these assumptions. My hope is to contribute to an evolving state of the art of non-profit assessment that over time will result in greater clarity.

One caution: Because of the diverse nature of client needs, wide variations in program services and differing perceptions about the needs and priorities of the larger society, I do not advise comparing the return on investment of one organization with another. Each of these 16 organizations in its own way offers an attractive return to its community, often exceeding what many would consider to be very acceptable for-profit investment performance.

Part I

IMPROVING TAXPAYER RETURNS IN EDUCATION,

COMMUNITY DEVELOPMENT, HUNGER ABATEMENT,

CORRECTIONS AND WELFARE DEPENDENCE

Motivating high school students to go to college,
thereby increasing their lifetime earnings

Admission Possible

Demographic projections show a decline in the number of college graduates over the next two decades. This has serious negative implications for the growth of the U.S. workforce. The only college-age population expected to grow over the next ten to twenty years is that of minority students, including African American and Hispanic students. Students from these populations come disproportionately from low-income families where parents likely did not attend college. This poses substantial barriers to their chances of going to college. The U.S. Department of Education reports that higher-income students who scored in the top third of a standardized test are five times more likely to attend college than lower-income students with comparable scores. The benefits of advancing more high-school students of color to a college education are substantial. The first to gain advantage are the students themselves who gain a lifetime earnings advantage of more than $1,000,000 over their non-college bound friends. Next are the employers who face a critical shortage of skilled workers over the next two decades. Finally taxpayers gain as students become taxpayers and enhance their incomes through career advancement.

Admission Possible was founded in September 2000 to enable students who had never envisioned a college education the opportunity of developing the skills needed to gain admission to a four year B.A.- degree institution. The organization began by serving 35 students in the Twin Cities and now serves 1,400 low-income high school juniors and seniors annually in the metropolitan area. It has had a remarkable record in a short time and is an excellent candidate for the application of a return-on-investment formula. Low income families offer a rich untapped source

4

of future college graduates because historically their rate of college attendance has been very low and demographically their anticipated future growth rate is comparatively high. Typically children from these families have little chance of going to college without intervention by a caring and knowledgeable third party. The cost of successfully mentoring these students, the increased probability of their gaining college admission and graduation and the significantly increased lifetime earnings accorded to college graduates are key inputs in determining the return on investment of this type of civic commitment.

By investing in Admission Possible the philanthropic investor can provide Minnesota taxpayers with a 53% return on investment ($1.53 for each $1.00 invested) by the fifth year of a college graduate's employment, by the tenth year a 163% return and over 40 years of work a 333% rate of return ($4.33 for each $1.00 invested).

MANAGEMENT

Jim McCorkell is the founder and chief executive officer of Admission Possible. Having grown up in a hard-working lower-income family, he has a keen appreciation of the challenges facing children whose parents have had a limited educational experience. He excelled as a student graduating cum laude from Carlton College and earning his M.A. in Political Science from the University of North Carolina. In June of 1999 he received his Masters of Public Education degree from Harvard University where his concentration was in the strategic management of public and nonprofit organizations with a complementary focus on education, race, poverty and gender. He returned to Minnesota in 2000 to found Admission Possible. McCorkell says, "I have come to the conclusion that one of the single most powerful levers in American society is increasing access to higher education." Since its founding more than 3,000 students have been assisted with 98% earning admission to college. Over $12 million has been raised from individuals ($3.4 million), corporate ($3.6 million) and private foundations ($5.0 million). McCorkell supervises a full- time staff of 85 and has recruited a 20-member Board of Directors. The board is diverse with representation from Fortune 500 companies, leading financial institutions, secondary and higher education, a private foundation, alumni and community volunteers.

ORGANIZATIONAL STRUCTURE

Reporting to McCorkell are the director of external relations who oversees coordinators for development and communications and the chief operating officer whose direct reports include coordinators for operations, expansion and programs. The program director oversees six coordinators who manage the activities at the nineteen schools currently served. Assisting these coordinators are fifty-two AmeriCorps and four VISTA members. In addition an executive director, two full-time staff and 12 AmeriCorps and VISTA members run the program for the Milwaukee area. Working with 19 high schools in the Twin Cities metro region Admission Possible annually delivers its two year program to more than 1,400 high-school juniors and seniors from low income families providing them with the tools necessary to gain admission to college. Critical services offered include: SAT and ACT test preparation, intensive guidance in preparing college applications and help in obtaining financial aid and support in transitioning to college. Average family income for Admission Possible families is $25,000. 93% are students of colors and 60% are female. 33% are Hmong, 18% African American, 19% African Immigrant, 9% Latino, 7% Multi Racial/Biracial/Other, 7% White, 6% Asian (Non-Hmong) and 1% Native American.

Admission Possible utilizes AmeriCorps "coaches" to deliver its services. These full-time mentors, who work with teams of ten to fifteen students at each high school, provide personal coaching. Coaches meet with the same group of juniors and seniors two afternoons per week for two hours. Maryam Ayir and Christopher TunBaw were St. Paul high school students who worked with their Admission Possible coach Ben Pierson through their senior year of high school. Maryam says, "The relationship I have with my coach is really comfortable. I don't really see him as an adult who intimidates me or that I can't go to. I can go to Ben for anything!" Adds Chris, "My coach is great. He is one of the most amazing people I have ever met. He is willing to help me out with everything." Students participate in a total of about 320 hours over two years on group ACT preparation, group admissions and financial aid counseling, one-on-one admissions and financial aid consulting visits. Personal coaching continues over the summer with students expected to apply for a summer enrichment program. College graduates on average have lifetime earnings of $2,280,000 ($57,000/year) compared with high school degree diploma-only wage earners with lifetime earnings of $1,240,000 ($31,000/year).

TESTIMONIAL

Jessica Brooks is an Admission Possible program graduate who, after graduating college in 2009 with a degree in history, returned to Admission Possible as an AmeriCorps coach to her younger peers. Jessica credits Admission Possible not only for her college degree, but also for saving her life. Surrounded by gang activity as a teenager and growing up in a single-parent household with a mom working double shifts, Jessica was pushed to enroll in Admission Possible where she found a coach who believed in her. While her own counselor asked the private college to which Jessica applied to please honor her unqualified application, Jessica and her coach fought the stereotyping and tracking that so often happens to students without an advocate. Four years later, Jessica had a degree from Carleton College and a corporate opportunity she put on hold to return to Admission Possible where, as Jessica says, "I have a responsibility to help students in the way I was helped." Having now finished her year of service as a coach to Admission Possible students at Roosevelt High School, she begins her summer internship in human resources at Travelers Insurance on the path to a promising and productive professional career and as a future leader for the community.

CALCULATING THE RETURN ON INVESTMENT

Studies are available from numerous sources pointing out the financial advantage of a college education. Admission Possible has the benefit of a study conducted by the St. Paul, Minnesota based Wilder Foundation that documents the increased chances of a student gaining college acceptance as a result of their mentoring efforts. First, the cost per student successfully placed in college of about $3,000 is derived by dividing the entire annual budget of Admission Possible by the number of students placed. Next the financial advantage to taxpayers from one net student addition to higher education must be calculated. Studies show that the lifetime earnings of a college graduate are about $1,000,000 higher than for those only graduating from high school. Wilder Foundation research documents that Admission Possible students have a 48% higher chance of getting to college than non Admission Possible students.

The current graduation rate from Minnesota higher education institutions is 58% for all students. The estimated federal and state tax rate for Admission Possible graduates coming from lower income families is estimated at 15%. By taking the present value of the added lifetime earnings of an AP student, times the tax rate, times the 48% increased likelihood of college admittance, times the 58% Minnesota higher education graduation rate, we can derive the value added to taxpayers from the Admission Possible experience. This number divided by the cost per student successfully placed in college permits the ROI to be calculated. The Admission Possible budget is 75% funded by private philanthropic sources.

Assuming a 3.00% discount rate the investors in Admission Possible provide a 53% return to the community over five years ($4,600/$3,000), a 163% return over ten years and a 333% return over a forty year period ($13,000/$3,000).

The numbers do not reflect reduced medical and social costs associated with college graduates nor their added production and consumption value to the economy. Also not included in the analysis is any marginal cost to taxpayers for college tuition in the event that government subsidies are required. On the other hand likely offsetting these costs are the economic impact of the enhanced value of the production skills offered by a college education and the increased purchasing power from the attendant higher incomes of Admission Possible graduates.

ASSUMPTIONS:

(1) Cost per student placed in college (75% funded by private philanthropic sources) = $3,000

(2) Increased likelihood of college participation by an Admission Possible student = .48

(3) Graduation rate (6 years) for MN higher education institutions = .58

(4) Lifetime earnings of a USA high school graduate ($31,000/yr.) = $1,240,000

(5) Lifetime earnings of a USA BA degree college graduate ($57,000/yr.) = $2,280,000

	5 Years	10 Years	20 Years	40 Years
Earnings Gain from BA degree ($26,000/yr.)	$130,000	$260,000	$ 520,000	$1,040,000
US & MN Taxes Paid (Assume @ 15% rate)	$19,500	$39,000	$78,000	$156,000
Tax advantage from **Admission Possible** Students (.48 x .58)	$5,400	$10,800	$21,600	$43,200
Present Value @ 3%	$4,600	$7,900	$11,800	$13,000
ROI	53%	163%	293%	333%

(1) Admission Possible budget divided by successful annual placements; (2) Wilder Research Center, December, 2004; (3) Minnesota Measures, MN Office of Higher Education, February 2007; (4) & (5) Chronicle of Higher Education, April 2009.

CRITIQUE

The documentation regarding wage differentials among different levels of education is quite reliable, as are the numbers relating to college graduation rates. Because of Wilder Foundation's fine reputation, the numbers relating to the increased odds of an Admission Possible student gaining college acceptance are thought to be accurate. One might argue that Admission Possible might be "creaming" the very best of the available high-school students for college entrance. However, the program's growth in service to now 1,400 students annually decreases the likelihood that all participants could possibly be at the top of their class. Further evidence of this is the recorded average ACT score students achieve before entering the program. The baseline score of 14.5 (on a scale of 36 points) places students in the bottom tenth percent of all ACT test takers. Still, even if the claim of "creaming" were true, it might not alter the results much. It is likely that even the "very best" may have had no awareness that they could qualify academically or financially for college.

*Teaching prospective neighborhood
entrepreneurs how to start and bring their
small businesses to scale*

The Neighborhood
Development Center

The development of major regional commercial and retail centers outside urban residential neighborhoods has put traditional neighborhood small businesses at a competitive disadvantage. While beneficial in many ways, suburban development has removed much of the traditional leadership as well as the "walk to work" lifestyle of the past from the urban core. When legitimate neighborhood sensitive businesses leave the community, potential is ripe for gradual economic deterioration and the emergence of an unhealthy sub-culture that decides to earn its living any way it can.

What often results are concentrations of poverty, deteriorating schools, increased rates of crime and the continued exodus of middle class residents to more attractive neighborhoods. The taxpayer winds up footing the bill for a host of social services and criminal justice system responses that follow. The quality of life for the remaining urban residents declines and the workforce of the future is harmed by young people who fail to develop their full potential.

Well-managed community economic development programs can reverse these trends. One of the very early efforts to revive ailing commercial corridors in the Twin Cities was the success evidenced on Franklin Avenue in Minneapolis by the work of Brenda Draves and the American Indian Business Development Corporation. Currently one of the leading players in commercial and neighborhood revitalization is the Neighborhood Development Center. The benefits of this type of effort are many.

Twin City neighborhoods gain as new business activity generates jobs and the entrepreneurs managing these businesses bring stability and new leadership to the community. Minnesota taxpayers gain as tax revenue generated by these start up businesses more than offsets the cost of the initial investment by the fifth year of business.

One of the best-kept secrets in metropolitan centers is their hidden reservoir of entrepreneurial business talent. This coupled with the high concentration of low-income purchasing power documented by Michael Porter of Harvard suggests substantial untapped economic power in our urban centers. In the Twin Cities, Mike Temali and the Neighborhood Development Center (NDC) have learned how to identify, train, advise and assist in the financing of self-styled urban entrepreneurs. NDC alumni businesses have created over 2,000 jobs at a cost of $4,500 each and returned over $23 million annually to their own inner-city neighborhoods, according to Wilder Research of St. Paul, Minnesota.

The analysis that follows indicates that the philanthropic investor can deliver new tax revenue that returns 67% to the community by the end of the third year ($1.67 for each $1.00 invested). In terms of the volume of business generated by NDC client businesses Wilder Research concluded that going forward $18.00 of business activity is returned to the neighborhood for every additional net dollar invested.

Management

Executive director, Mike Temali has over twenty-five years of community economic development experience having managed agencies serving The Frogtown Summit-University, Payne-Phalen and Dayton's Bluff neighborhoods in St. Paul as well as the Central, Philips & Powderhorn and Hawthorne, Jordan & Near North neighborhoods in Minneapolis. He was retained by Western Bank's Chairman, William Sands, to develop the Neighborhood Development Center in 1990. Nearly 4,000 entrepreneurs have been assisted, and more than 500 new businesses the center has served are thriving today, creating more that $28 million in economic activity in the Twin Cities each year. The 14 members of the board of directors are leaders from business, community development centers, government, higher education and the foundation community.

Temali is a native of St. Paul who attended Macalester College and Gustavus Adolphus College completing his masters in public policy from the Humphrey Institute at the University of Minnesota. He is married and lives with his wife, son and daughter in St. Paul. His love of neighborhood and the support systems that were there for him at an early age may well be part of what motivates him to focus on re-energizing his community. Temali believes that, " supporting hundreds of small inner-city entrepreneurs is not only a tremendous way to build up a community's social and economic base, but their endless cultural diversity, business ideas, courage and energy are forever stimulating to be around."

ORGANIZATIONAL STRUCTURE

The center is structured with five leading program areas and a staff of 25 with an equal number of contract and volunteer trainers and consultants. *Micro-Enterprise Training* provides specialized training to Hmong, African American, Native American, Latino, Somali and East African entrepreneurs in their own languages where appropriate. Over a 16-week period the fundamentals of marketing, operations, financial management and development of a complete business plan are taught. *Small Business Loans and Islamically-Acceptable Reba-Free Financing* provides access to credit for start-up businesses unable to obtain funding from traditional sources of capital. *Satellite Business Resource Centers* provide on going support in marketing, merchandising, financial record keeping, credit repair, retail management and administrative support from five locations. In partnership with neighborhood organizations NDC reclaims and rehabs commercial properties that operate as *Small Business Incubators* to house and support local businesses. Through *Capacity Building* NDC assists 25 neighborhood partners to build their own capacity to generate economic development initiatives.

Through neighborhood surveys and community outreach NDC identifies potential entrepreneurs who may be operating micro enterprises out of their homes and who have the work ethic, technical skills and business ideas to start, maintain and grow a business. Micro-entrepreneur training is conducted in small classes with participants all from the same community. This creates a peer group that provides encouragement and support to one another as they explore becoming business owners. For many start-up businesses traditional funding sources are not an option. After successful completion of the NDC micro-entrepreneur training class, loans are available up to $20,000 for start-up businesses and up to $50,000 for growing businesses. In order to help entrepreneurs respond to changes and new challenges NDC provides experts to consult with business owners. More than 3,000 hours of technical assistance is provided each year. Six real estate developments such as the Midtown Global Market at the former Sears site on east Lake Street in south Minneapolis house over 120 businesses including start-ups and existing businesses owned by NDC training class alumni. This type of clustering offers new business owners easy access to the full range of NDC service

TESTIMONIAL

Jose Payan opened his tortilla factory in 1999 as a family operated business. LaPerla Tortilleria in 2009 had more than 50 employees at three locations: Payne Avenue, Mercado Central and south Minneapolis. His primary business is packaging and selling tortillas to local restaurants and grocery stores. Each of his locations is open to the public. LaPerla's products include corn and flour tortillas in all sizes made fresh, start to finish on site. He cooks and grinds his own flour, mixes ingredients, fries tostadas and tortilla chips and packages all products for shipment. Says Payan, "NDC helped me know exactly what I need to know to run a business, how to do taxes, payroll and how to write a good business plan."

COMPUTING THE RETURN ON INVESTMENT

Wilder Research of St. Paul MN conducted a comprehensive study of the Neighborhood Development Center in February 2008. The analysis covered NDC activity since inception, with financial return data focused on the period from 2000 to 2006. During this period, 3,780 entrepreneurs were assisted with one or more levels of NDC service. Wilder reviewed a list of 383 NDC clients that were still likely to be in business and of these 272 were surveyed. Businesses surveyed had an average of 3.0 employees, which together with the 383 business owners resulted in 1,522 new jobs created.

The Wilder study documented that for the year 2006 the 383 existing businesses on average generated the following economic activity. Rent $3,209,917; general business expense (excluding rent and payroll) $5,928,909; payments to subcontractors 1,961,809 and payroll $14,207,469; payroll taxes of all business owners $2,342,321; property taxes paid of $170,931 and sales taxes of $693,872. I have estimated that additional second-phase taxes of $1,400,000 were paid by NDC employees and venders. In total more than $25,000,000 of economic activity was generated and nearly $4,600,000 of taxes were paid in 2006. 86% of surveyed business owners received training from NDC; 33% financing, 28% training from the Business and Career Center and 17% had a location in an NDC incubator. 37% of surveyed owners started a new business and 63% expanded a pre-existing business. A typical business is a sole proprietorship with one location serving customers living within one mile of their business.

For purposes of computing the return on investment for NDC it is assumed that $7,090,634 of program expenses from 2000 to 2006 was spent over a six year period. The next step is to calculate the benefits provided to the Minnesota tax payer. Payroll taxes of $2,342,321, property taxes of $170,931 and sales taxes of $693,872 are paid each year. It is assumed that an additional $1,400,000 in taxes is collected each year from the general economic activity of the 383 businesses estimated to still be in business. Total estimated taxes generated each year are $4,600,000 or a total of $9,200,000 over two years which means break-even is achieved about midway through the second year.

The six-year cost of $7.1 million is more than offset by taxes collected by the end of the second year. Each year thereafter generates at least an additional $4.6 million of taxes or the equivalent of a 67% rate of return on the initial investment of $7.1 million by the end of the third year.

Wilder estimates that the annual net additional investment by NDC (estimated at $788,000) generates eighteen dollars of spending in the community for each one dollar invested. It is assumed that while some businesses may fail in future years others will prosper and offset prospective losses. The assumptions used are thought to be conservative. Also since 57% of all business owners did not report payroll tax information it is likely that the tax contribution for payroll taxes is understated.

ASSUMPTIONS:

Total Program Expense 2000-2006 = $7,090,634
Cost (2000-2006) Per Entrepreneur Served in 2007 = $2,919
Cost (2000-2006) Per Current Business in 2007 = $18,513
Cost (2000-2006) Per Current Job in 2007 = $4,658

Dollars returned to the Community in 2006

Dollars returned to the community	3 years	5 years	10 years	15 years	20 years
Rent ($3.2mm)	$9.6	$16.0	$32.0	$48.0	$64.0
Other business expenses ($5.9mm)	$17.7	$29.5	$59.0	$88.5	$118.0
Payroll ($14.2mm)	$42.6	$71.0	$142.0	$213.0	$248.0
Subcontractor expenses ($2.0mm)	$6.0	$10.0	$20.0	$30.0	$40.0
Total $ returned ($25.3)	$75.9	$126.5	$253.0	&379.5	$506.0
Present Value at 5%	$65.6	$99.0	$155.3	$182.5	$190.7

Taxes Generated in 2006	3 years	5 years	10 years	15 years	20 years
Sales tax ($.7mm)	$2.1	$3.5	$7.0	$10.5	$14.1
Other taxes ($1.4mm)	$4.2	$7.0	$14.0	$21.0	$28.0
Payroll taxes ($2.3mm)	$6.9	$11.5	$23.0	$35.4	$46.0
Property taxes ($0.2mm)	$.6	$1.0	$2.0	$3.0	$4.0
Total taxes ($4.6)	$13.8	$23.0	$46.0	&69.0	$92.0
Present Value at 5%	$11.9	$18.0	$128.2	$33.2	$34.7

Note: The "Other Taxes" in the table above assumes that Other Business Expense of $5.9 million, Sub-contractor payments of $2.0 million and Rent paid of $3.2 million each year for a total of $11.1 million in annual expenditures by NDC businesses generate an additional $1,100,000 in taxes annually by others equivalent to a rate of 10% (sales tax, individual and business income tax and added real estate taxes). It also assumes that in addition to payroll taxes the $14.2 million annual payroll of NDC businesses generates added taxes of $300,000 annually by others (at a rate of 2%) as the dollars flow through the system impacting sales, income and real estate taxes. If the assumed benefit from Other Taxes was eliminated from the calculation break-even would occur midway through the third year with a 65% return on the initial investment of $7.1 million earned each year thereafter.

CRITIQUE

Without an experienced evaluation process developed over the years by the Wilder Foundation of St. Paul, this type of analysis could not have been completed. The skills involved are many: in terms of knowing how to access data, organize it and derive appropriate conclusions that are credible. This type of model clearly has application to those who take on the task of revitalizing neighborhoods and commercial corridors. It is especially appropriate in these times, when our urban centers, which have been under siege for many years, are showing renewed vitality—assisted in part by the entrepreneurial skills of new immigrants. It would appear logical for policy makers and government officials to insure that the skills necessary for this type of community development evaluation were present in each of our major urban and rural centers.

*Large-scale voluntary food shelf distribution systems
reduce the cost of hunger in the USA*

Second Harvest Heartland

It is estimated that nearly 35 million Americans are hungry enough each day to damage their physical, mental and emotional health. Currently the federal government spends nearly $50 billion a year on nutrition programs (food stamps $33 billion, school lunches $10 billion; WIC $5 billion & other $2 billion). This is about $12 million short of the amount that some experts estimate would close the hunger gap in the U.S.A. Food stamps generally meet about 20 days of family monthly needs for those who participate in the program. Food shelves generally cover another 4 to 5 days, with families in many cases not able to finance the remaining 5 to 6 days of the month.

In Minnesota only 57% of those eligible participate in the food stamp program. Time constraints, transportation problems, lack of knowledge and pride all limit usage. Family members have been known to drive to neighboring counties in rural areas to register in order to avoid the stigma of poverty in their local community. The Sodexho Foundation study of June 5, 2007 estimates the burden (impact cost) of domestic hunger to our economy to be $76 billion dollars each year or $2,170 per individual going without sufficient food. The estimated $76 billion cost to our economy from families going hungry is comprised of impaired educational outcomes for children and medical costs for all family members, including both mental and physical issues that must be dealt with at clinics and hospitals.

Second Harvest Heartland is the leading provider of food and services to the food banks which serve Minnesota and western Wisconsin's low-income populations. It is estimated that Second Harvest Heartland meets about 14% of the monthly food needs of nearly 150,000 needy people, for a projected cost savings to the economy of $304 per person served. In 2008 the agency distributed 41 million pounds of food. Nine dollars in food value can be generated by every $1 invested in Second Harvest Heartland.

There are at least two ways to calculate the ROI of an investment in SHH. First is the simple calculation that $1 invested generates $9 of food to needy persons. The second is to calculate the estimated $304 per capita that is saved serving 150,000 people for a total savings of $45.6 million to the economy. On this basis the $8.4 million of annual investment in SHH would generate better than a 400% return on investment ($5 gained for every $1 invested).

MANAGEMENT

Executive director, Robert Zeaske joined Second Harvest Heartland in 2008 after a 13-year career with both for-profit and non-profit organizations. He has a distinguished career in marketing and sales, personnel recruitment, performance measurement analytics, fundraising and general management. Prior to coming to Second Harvest Heartland he served as senior vice president for "Jumpstart for Young Children" a nationally recognized early literacy organization where he led private fund raising, the marketing of public policy and corporate relations. He is a graduate of Stanford University and earned his MBA at the Harvard Business School.

Zeaske is motivated by a sense of deep gratitude for the benefits this country has provided to him and his family. He is a believer in the significant role that non-profits play in the social and economic fabric of this country. Zeaske is zealous about instilling best practices in non-profit management and applying the metrics that permits candid evaluation of results. The 18 members of the board of directors includes representatives from the food industry (Cargill/General Mills/SuperValu/Target/ Cub Foods), consumer, industrial products, and distribution companies (Ecolab/ 3M/Optimum Health/Minnesota Trucking Association), finance and marketing (Bremer Financial/Ceridian/Padilla Speer Beardsley Public Relations/Larsen Allen Accounting/Merrill Lynch/Information Builders) and others from government and the community including a representative from Sodexo USA, the foundation that commissioned the "Economic Cost of Domestic Hunger USA" research study.

ORGANIZATIONAL STRUCTURE

The Second Harvest management team is structured with a chief operating officer reporting to Rob Zeaske who oversees directors of food bank operations, field services, food sourcing and human resources.

Also reporting to Zeaske are the vice presidents for advancement, new initiatives, external relations, the controller and an executive assistant.

The organization is dedicated to ending hunger through community partnerships as well as increasing public awareness of hunger. SHH obtains, stores and distributes donated and purchased food to member agencies (churches/neighborhood organizations) and directly to low-income individuals in Minnesota and western Wisconsin.

Second Harvest Heartland distributes 41 million pounds of food per year or enough to feed the entire city of Chaska, Minnesota, for one year. SHH estimates the wholesale market value of a basket of food at $1.69 per pound or the equivalent of nearly $70,000,000 of purchasing power distributed each year. The average person using a food shelf needs an estimated 234 pounds per year of supplemental food after using their food stamps and their own money. This totals about $395 per person or in excess of $1,000 for a family of three per year. On average, food shelf users make six visits per year and take home 39 pounds per visit. The average annual family benefit from food stamps is about $2,250 which together with the $1,067 average benefit from food shelf services makes it possible for low income families (often less than $12,000 per year of income) to meet other critical needs.

TESTIMONIAL

"I would love to say thank you to everyone who put this organization together. Without people like you, this world would be a much harder place to live in for all of us, especially in hard times like this. I'm a single mother of two. I lost my companion and the father of my two children almost seven years ago to a murder. Life has been a hard struggle for us. I didn't get laid off, I had to resign due to medical reasons, but thinking I was going to get my job back, and didn't. So again I want to thank you so much for everything you've done not just for me and my family, but for each individual family that you put meals on their table. I don't have the words to thank you. I never heard of this offering before, but I know soon I will be back on my feet again, and will make a contribution in return, or if you ever need volunteers, I would be honored to help. Thank you." Nicole R.

CALCULATING THE RETURN ON INVESTMENT

In calculating the return on an investment in SHH the first step is to calculate the annual investment required to generate the amount of food distributed each year. For SHH this number consists of government grants of $1.9MM, foundation and corporate grants of $1.9MM, general contributions of $2.4MM, United Way of $.6MM and reinvested earned program income of $1.5MM for a total of $8.4MM. This investment generates $69.3MM of food distributed each year at wholesale and $82 MM at retail or in effect $9 of retail sales for every $1 invested.

The next step is to attempt to determine what SHH's contribution is to the savings to the economy and taxpayer that researchers estimate comes from a reduction in hunger. This involves a number of assumptions one of which is that SHH's Minnesota experience is similar to the nations overall experience as illustrated in the study completed by "The Sodexho Foundation in partnership with the Public Welfare Foundation and Spunk Fund, Inc." dated June 5, 2007.

This analysis of the economic cost of hunger estimates that exclusive of the impact of charity, hunger costs America $76 Billion annually. The key cost components are illness and psychosocial dysfunction $66.8 Billion and impaired education and lowered worker productivity $9.2 Billion. The Sodexho study estimates that approximately 35 million Americans are impaired by the lack of enough food in their daily diet. Using these assumptions the annual cost to the economy of each "hungry" person is projected to be $2,171.

SHH serves nearly 150,000 people each year, meeting 4 to 5 days of their monthly food requirements after food stamps and cash purchases (about 14%). The estimated per capita annual savings to the economy from SHH'S services can be computed by multiplying 14% times $ 2,171, or $304 per person served. This brings the total savings to the economy ($304 x 150,000 people served) to $45.6MM. This total savings number divided by the $8.4MM invested in SHH each year equates to a better than a 400% return after recapturing the original investment of $8.4MM.

Return per dollar of Sales = $4.33

$36.4MM Value of Food Distributed

$8.4MM Annual Investment

Return per dollar of Investment = $5.43

$45.6 MM Est. Economic Savings by SHH

$8.4 MM Annual Investment

Assumptions:

Americans impacted by hunger each year= 35MM

Total annual cost burden of hunger in America= $76MM

% of client's monthly food requirements met by SHH= 14%

Clients served annually by SHH= 150,000

The economic cost of hunger for SHH clients approximates that calculated by the Sodexho study of June, 2007

Adverse Outcome (Health)	2005 Direct/Indirect Costs
Migraines	$1.7 Billion
Colds	0.4
Iron deficiency	0.2
Depression	15.6
Anxiety	9.2
Suicide	6.4
Upper gastrointestinal tract disorder	2.5
Other hospitalization	7.1
Excess cost of other fair or poor health status	23.7
Subtotal:	**$ 66.8 Billion**
Adverse Outcome (Education/Productivity)	
Absenteeism	$4.2
Grade retention (drop out)	5.0
Subtotal:	**$9.2 Billion**
Total Cost	**$76.0 Billion**

CRITIQUE

Key assumptions are that the costs of hunger in America based on the comprehensive "Sodexho" study are conservative, and that this national data can be applied to citizens served by SHH. It is helpful that authors of the report are highly qualified leaders in their field and include Dr. J. Larry Brown, Harvard School of Public Health; Dr. Donald Shepard, Brandeis University; Dr. Timothy Martin, Brandeis University; and Dr. John Orwat, Loyola University. It would be logical for individual state elected officials to fund studies that test the "Sodexho" conclusions.

Reducing the recidivism rate
for juvenile offenders

Osiris Program

Americans are becoming more aware of the rising cost of criminal behavior by our youth, as well as of creative new corrections programs to reduce their rate of recidivism. For example, in any given year as many as 400 youth offenders, 86% with felony convictions, may reside at the Hennepin County Home School for youthful offenders located in Minnetonka, Minnesota. Sixty-three percent have already been in other facilities before coming to the Hennepin County Home School. Approximately 70% of serious teen offenders have a mental health diagnosis, with significant behavioral problems and chemical dependency issues. Many private facilities, nonprofits and even hospitals will not accept teens with these challenges. Only a few accept girls. HCHS takes on all these issues. A recent standardized assessment of residents indicated that 73.5% were thought to be at high risk to re-offend. Many of the residents of HCHS are of employment age but lack the skills and know-how needed to enter and remain employed in today's computer literate society. It costs taxpayers between $70,000 and $80,000 per year for one youth in residence at HCHS, at a cost of $250 per day for an average stay of 9 months.

The Osiris Program illustrates the positive return to the community from programs that creatively teach technical, life and employment placement skills at the Hennepin County Home School. Bill and Gail Roddy started the program in 1997. Their work has reduced the recidivism rate at Hennepin County Home School and brought former residents into the workforce after supplying them with a broad range of advanced computer skills. Twin City neighborhoods have benefitted from Osiris because graduates reintegrate back into the neighborhood becoming part of "the solution" with new found social and computer skills. In addition Minnesota businesses can draw from a larger pool of motivated workers with high-tech skills and compete more effectively in the world wide economy.

Minnesota taxpayers also gain as social service and criminal justice system costs are reduced through lower rates of recidivism and as $8.00 to $12.50 per hour jobs add to the tax base.

Philanthropic and government investors can deliver returns up to and exceeding 400% ($5 earned for each $1 invested) to the community by investing in this program. The benefit to the county and state is very large in terms of both dollars and quality of life.

MANAGEMENT

Bill and Gail Roddy gained their business skills from managing two successful network marketing companies starting in the 1980s. Bill recalls mentors from his days in Chicago who assisted his athletic career and kept him focused on the long-term advantages of a good academic background. He has a bachelors degree in business from the University of St Thomas. Gail received her bachelors degree in psychology and sociology from the University of Minnesota. Following college she worked as a counselor in adolescent counseling centers. Both Gail and Bill feel that they have been blessed in many ways and the formation of Osiris was a way of utilizing their business skills to assist youth from troubled backgrounds. Bill and Gail Roddy are Osiris only full-time employees. They contract with one full-time life skills counselor who provides direct service to the youth and one technical support person for the community computer centers. Interestingly, the technical support person is a 30-year-old graduate of Osiris who has been with the program since he was 15. Gail and Bill are on the Osiris board along with a property management company owner, a health products business owner, a marketing director from Wells Fargo Home Mortgage and banker from Wells Fargo Private Client Services.

ORGANIZATIONAL STRUCTURE

On average Osiris works with about 30% or 133 of the approximately 400 youth that enter and exit HCHS in any given year. Of these 133 youth, about 80%, or about 100, complete the Osiris computer, life skills and employment training program. It is estimated that 70% of the program participants successfully transition off probation and do not re-offend. Each year about 30 of the youth who complete computer training are provided with a six- month adult supervised employment position as youth instructors in the Minneapolis Park and Recreation Board public parks. This follows their exit from HCHS and assists with their reintegration back into the community. The cost per youth instructor is $4,305 for six months, requiring a commitment of 20 hours per week, for a total cost of about $130,000 per year. It is estimated that 85% of youth computer instructors successfully transition off probation and do not re-offend as a result of skills acquired and continued support from youth counselors. The potential for expansion is great. Added funding for more youth instructors could enable Minneapolis Parks and Recreation Board to facilitate Osiris building a total of 36 community computer centers in the parks to complement the existing infrastructure of 17 community computer centers. Expansion to 36 computer centers in the Minneapolis public parks would provide a total of 144 youth with after school employment in their communities.

TESTIMONIAL

Henry Sharpe, age 28, is a U.S. Air Force veteran, a college student and dynamic CEO of Sharpe Solutions, a personal computer installation and trouble shooting business. Sharpe, a former juvenile offender and Osiris alumnus, recalls advice from a former HCHS counselor, "I've seen guys like you before and you need to take a look inside." Sharpe did and the results speak for themselves.

CALCULATING THE RETURN ON INVESTMENT

On a conservative basis it is estimated that hard-core juvenile offenders can cost the state and county $70,000 per year in counseling, housing, education and other custodial services. With an HCHS recidivism rate that averages about 50% for hard core juvenile offenders, the return on investment is high when this rate can be reduced to 30% or in some cases as low as 15%. Social service costs to families with offending juveniles drop dramatically when former delinquents straighten out their lives, and the government also collects more taxes from them.

Hennepin County Corrections estimates that the Osiris Organization computer, life skills and employment training program has a positive impact on the recidivism rate reducing it by 20 percentage points (or 30% rate) for the 100 youth completing the program. This amounts to an annual savings for taxpayers of $1,400,000 per year (20 percentage points times 100 youth times $70,000 in annual savings).

The County also estimates that the 30 youth who go on to complete the six-month paid youth instructor internship program have an even greater reduction in recidivism, amounting to an additional 15 percentage points (or 15% rate). This provides taxpayers with added savings of $315,000 per year.

A minimum of 25 youth who complete the six month internship wind up being placed in jobs that pay between $8.00 and $12.00 per hour totaling on average $142,000 in annual earnings for the group. This provides modest added tax revenues for the state of Minnesota and the USA (not included in the calculations).

These annual savings to Minnesota taxpayers amount to a minimum of $1,715,000 per year. Osiris has an annual budget of $350,000 which means that the taxpayer benefits exceed their costs by more than five times or a one year return on investment exceeding 400%.

Assumptions:

Osiris annual budget = $350,000
Cost Per Placement at HCHS for 9 Mos. = $70,000
Average Recidivism Rate = 50%
Recidivism Rate for Osiris HCSC Training Graduates = 30%
Recidivism Rate for Osiris Six Month Paid Teacher Mentoring = 15%

Per Year	HCHS annual population	Youth entering Osiris	Youth completing program	Youth completing teaching
Number of youth	400	133	100	30
Estimated recidivism rate	50%	50%	30%	15%
Reduction in recidivism rate	none	none	20%	15%
Resultant savings	none	none	$1,400,000	$315,000

CRITIQUE

The Osiris Organization program analysis requires that assumptions be made about the amount that taxpayer expenses decline from reduced recidivism, as well as the gain in tax revenue to the state of Minnesota accruing from the advanced computer skills taught in the program. We have excluded the expected gain in tax revenues because the savings from reduced recidivism are so large. However, the long term benefits from moving a former juvenile offender into the world of work should be very large. The state of the art must evolve further if more precise measures of ROI are to benefit Minnesota investors and taxpayers. For example, tracking the history of HCSC graduates to determine whether they re-offend and are incarcerated in other counties or states would provide a more accurate measure of the true rate of recidivism. Other variables not easily tracked would include the years of continued employment and wage level gains, five and ten years into the future after graduation from HCHS.

*Working off of welfare and moving
out of poverty with tax credits*

AccountAbility Minnesota

The Earned Income Tax Credit (EITC) is a federal tax credit for working individuals and families whose incomes range from well below the poverty line to about double the poverty line ($14,000 for a family of two and $17,600 for a family of three). By restricting eligibility to families with earnings, the Earned Income Tax Credit promotes work. It is the largest federal aid program targeting the working poor and is credited for significantly increasing the number of single parents in the workforce. The EITC represents up to a 40% increase in income for some workers. It can turn an $8.00 per hour job into an $11.00 per hour job. The Brookings Institution has called the Earned Income Tax Credit (EITC) the nation's most effective anti-poverty program, lifting an average of 4.4 million Americans above the poverty level each year. A Brookings Institution study found that 60% of the increase between 1984 and 1996 in the percentage of women with children who work (73% in 1984 and 81% by 1996) was attributable to the Earned Income Tax Credit. The US economy and industry in general benefit by new additions to the workforce who become both producers and consumers. US taxpayers claim a double benefit through reduced welfare expense and increased tax receipts. Poverty is reduced in communities across the USA. This brings improved quality of life to our neighborhoods manifested by reduced rates of crime, less homelessness and children better prepared to learn in school.

An IRS study estimates that only 75 to 80% of eligible households claim the EITC and that up to $8 billion in EITC refunds went unclaimed in 2008. In addition according to a Brookings report of 2007, 61% of all Minnesota EITC filers paid to have their returns prepared. These services can be costly. A fee of $120 or more is typical and amounts to a significant subtraction from the average EITC receipt of $1,746 for the year 2007. Refund anticipation loans (RALs) allow EITC filers to receive funds 8-10 days sooner than if they chose to have their credits direct deposited to a bank account. Many families choose RALs because they don't have the funds on hand to pay for the tax preparation fee. The interest rate on RALs is $100 or more, which computes to an average annualized interest rate of 236%. For the nation, the IRS estimated that $1.9 billion of EITC money intended for low-income families flowed instead to tax preparation and interest charges in 2004. In Minnesota that total was $24 million.

Minnesota low-income wage earners also can benefit from a comparable program called the Working Family Tax Credit. In addition, workers who earn more that $3,000 (reduced from $8,500) can qualify for the Child Tax Credit for up to $1,000 per child.

Leaders in the accounting profession organized this Twin Cities nonprofit in the mid-1970s, first to assist small organizations and businesses, and later to help low-income families prepare tax returns and specifically take advantage of the cash refunds offered by the "Earned Income Tax Credit." This tax program evolved from bi-partisan leaders in Congress, who in 1975 recognized the merits of devising a means of encouraging low-income individuals to achieve self-sufficiency. In 2010 AccountAbility Minnesota generated $35.6 million in tax refunds to Minnesotans serving more than 19,000 low-income taxpayers and completing more than 44,000 federal and state tax returns.

By investing in AccountAbility Minnesota, philanthropic investors can deliver an immediate annual return of 60% and higher to the state ($1.60 for each $1.00 invested).

These benefits are derived from reduced social service expense, increased taxes paid and additions to the work force of previously unemployed welfare recipients. For example: If the EITC motivates a worker to move from $8.00/hour to $12.00/hour the savings to the taxpayer are about $8,800 per worker, according to the 2002 study by the Minnesota Legislative Auditor. AAM's annual budget of about $900,000 generated $25 million in refunds returned to Minnesota workers/consumers in 2009. Many individuals on welfare and certain low wage workers evidently feel an increased incentive to work, knowing in advance that their support from government may decline, but will not be eliminated entirely as their income increases.

ORGANIZATIONAL STRUCTURE

AccountAbility Minnesota (AAM) provides free comprehensive tax assistance and related financial services year-round to a diverse population of low-income and other underserved residents of Minnesota. Over 65% of clients served are from communities of color. AAM is the only community-based nonprofit organization in the state with a mission solely devoted to free tax assistance and financial services that encourage taxpayers to use their cash refunds to build assets and long-term financial security. In 2010 more than 8,000 children benefited from the tax refunds and nearly 800 volunteers gave 27,132 hours to prepare the 44,000 returns.

Thirteen permanent staff persons handle daily operations and manage hundreds of volunteers who make the organization's free tax assistance possible. Volunteers ensure that the tax sites offer high quality service serving as: Tax Screeners, Individual Tax Preparers, Small Business Tax Preparers, Quality Reviewers, Financial Planners and Interpreters who are multilingual. AAM estimates that it saves hundreds of low income people nearly $300 each on tax preparation and refund anticipation loan fees each year. Services are provided at thirteen sites in the Twin Cities. Partnering with fifteen greater-Minnesota organizations clinics is hosted at an additional twenty-two sites.

Additionally, during the tax season AAM hires a team of seasonal employees: ten to fifteen part-time Tax Site Managers to operate the community tax sites; six to eight financial services specialists to implement AAM's Express Refund Loan and Savings Program; and one electronic tax file coordinator to manage the thousands of electronic tax returns filed from the main office. Staff is diverse and represents the following communities: African 15%, African American 19%, Asian 19%, Caucasian 40% and Latino/Hispanic 7%.

MANAGEMENT

Tracy Fishman joined AAM as Executive Director in July 2009 with more than seventeen years of experience in public policy and community based services. She served as vice president for public policy at Planned Parenthood in Illinois and worked for the Chicago Department of Public Health's STD/HIV/AIDS Division. She has served on numerous Chicago foundation, health advocacy and public policy boards. She holds a bachelor's degree from Macalester College and a master's degree in public policy from the Harris School of Public Policy in Chicago. Her immediate predecessor, Bonnie Esposito, served as Executive Director of AAM from 2002 to 2009. Esposito designed and implemented community-based volunteer and community service programs for over twenty-five years. Her programs involved state and municipal government, community action agencies and corporations in Minnesota, Michigan, Connecticut, Pennsylvania, New York and Wisconsin.

The staff work closely with both the Internal Revenue Service and the Minnesota Department of Revenue to establish training classes and to develop effective learning models that are adapted to volunteers' unique levels of expertise. A board of twelve directors governs the agency which includes representatives from Delta Airlines, Wells Fargo, Target, Best Buy, US Bank, Northway Community Trust, West Side Safe Neighborhood Council, KMPG-LLP, Frederickson & Byron-P.A., Bethel University, Lutheran Social Service and CBIZ/Mayer Hoffman McCann P.C.

TESTIMONIALS

"I am so thankful for AccountAbility Minnesota," Brenda Coleman explains. "I need this refund because I've been in transitional housing for over four years. I just received a Section 8 voucher in December and I just moved into my own apartment. I need to begin with a good start and this refund will help me pay some bills and stay ahead by putting some monies aside. My son has worked extremely hard this year so he can graduate on time. I am so proud of him. I love him so much and I want him to have the best graduation ever. Also I want him to put something aside for when he gets ready to go to college this fall."

Priscilla Kar filed her taxes for free with AccountAbility Minnesota this year after learning about the services through a co-worker. Ms. Kar is a 26 year old single mom with one child. This year she had combined federal and state tax refunds of over $4,000. Savings is very important for Ms. Kar because she plans to buy her own house after graduation and also pay for her daughter's education in the future. Prior to filing her taxes with AAM she was unable to open an account with a bank. Through the agency's Express Refund Loan and Savings Program, she was able to open a standard savings account with US Federal Credit Union. "It was the best part of this whole experience for me," says Ms. Kar explaining the importance of finally being able to access a mainstream financial institution. She plans on opening up a CD or other savings products so that she can watch her money grow for herself and her daughter.

CALCULATING THE RETURN ON INVESTMENT

The Center on Budget and Policy Priorities in Washington D.C. reports that census data indicates that in 2003, the Earned Income Tax Credit lifted 4.4 million people out of poverty including 2.4 million children. That is equivalent to 1.47% of the US population of an estimated 300 million people. Applying that same percentage to Minnesota's population of about 5.0 million would mean that approximately 73,500 Minnesotans were lifted out of poverty in 2003. Since the average family size in Minnesota is 3.09 members, an estimated 24,000 families may have been lifted out of poverty by the EITC in 2003. According to the Children's Defense Fund-Minnesota, 242,000 lower income Minnesota working families benefited from the EITC in 2004. This would imply that if the patterns remain close to the same each year that a minimum of about 10% of Minnesota's EITC recipient families were lifted above the poverty level in 2003.

AccountAbility Minnesota (AAM) served 17,250 taxpayers in 2009. Applying the 10% factor to AAM taxpayers served in 2009 results in about 1,725 taxpayers or an estimated 860 families (averaging 2.0 persons per family) having been raised out of poverty that year. The assumption is that a minimum of 10% of AAM's clients would not otherwise have known to file for the EITC. The poverty rate for a family of two was about $14,000 in 2009 or the equivalent of earning nearly $6.75 per hour.

Assuming the lift out of poverty was a modest gain from $7.00 to $8.00 per hour, the resulting savings in federal and state expense would amount to about $2,400 per family according to the Minnesota Legislative Auditors Study illustrating cash and non-cash resources at various employment and wage levels (See Appendix 5). Because we are assuming an average size of 2.0 persons per family for AAM a 30% discount has been applied to the net benefit derived from the Auditors Table which assumes a family size of 3.0 persons. The resultant savings would be about $1,680 per family. This assumes that the family took advantage of the entire range of benefits provided by government.

Applying this amount to the estimated 860 families raised out of poverty by AccountAbility Minnesota (AAM) means that in 2009 alone AAM saved federal and state government and their taxpayers at least $1,448,000. This savings exceeds the AAM annual budget of approximately $900,000 by more than 1.6 times for an equivalent return on investment of 60%. The savings increase dramatically as families increase their earning power, and are even more substantial when a previously unemployed individual moves to an $8.00 per hour job or higher.

CRITIQUE

The state of the art must evolve further to develop more precise measures of AAM's ROI. A longitudinal study comparing EITC benefits received by AAM and non-AAM clients would be very helpful. Tracking the wage patterns of EITC recipients from their non-working status to employment at each $2.00/hour increment of the wage scale would add credibility to the "motivation to work" issue associated with the EITC. It is possible that simulation exercises with unemployed individuals on welfare might shed more light on what triggers a change in attitude towards work. In addition it should be in state government's self interest to update annually tables such as the Legislative Auditors Study so that more current and accurate analysis can be made about assistance programs that encourage the transition from welfare to work.

Part II

CREATIVE APPROACHES TO RAISING THE

PRODUCTIVITY OF INVESTMENTS IN HOUSING

AFFORDABLE TO FAMILIES OF ALL AGES

Housing was no longer affordable for many Americans even prior to the current recession. Minnesota has about 45% of households that rent (230,000) and 28.7% of home owners (446,000) paying more than 30% of their income for housing. Of these, 115,000 renters and 140,000 homeowners pay more than 50% of their incomes for housing. Currently about 75% of Minnesota residents own their own homes and 25% rent. Shedding some light on the problem is the fact that for the period 2001-2007 median gross rents (including utilities) increased 12% while median renter income gained only 4%. For the same period median home prices rose 34% while household income gained only 12%. When families have to pay more than 30% of their income for housing, the family is stressed financially. Families often move frequently which in turn impacts school performance, job performance, child care costs and transportation logistics. Less costly substandard housing impacts family health and stability, results in overcrowding and often increases the chances of criminal justice system involvement. Roughly 10,000 Minnesotans are homeless according to the Minnesota Housing Partnership and nearly 40% of these are children and youth.

It generally requires about $60,000 of income to purchase a home, which means that many school teachers and police officers must rent. To rent a two-bedroom apartment requires nearly $30,000 of income which is beyond the affordability of most retail sales people and food preparation workers. Estimates vary, but there is a sense among experts that Minnesota needs a minimum of about 35,000 new units of affordable housing to improve the imbalance between supply and demand. The Minneapolis based Family Housing Fund estimates that more than 170,000 existing cost burdened households need assistance through new construction, additional vouchers and new rental assistance.

Closing this substantial gap in affordable workforce housing will require more public investment, the preservation of existing subsidized units, reduced demolitions and reduced regulatory barriers. More private, philanthropic and government investment in creative new approaches that combine housing with supportive services will be essential to raising family incomes and reducing housing costs. There is a continuum of needs in affordable housing, beginning with supportive housing which deals with the homeless, subsidized rental for those receiving some form of support, standard rental, subsidized ownership and finally standard home ownership. The next five studies cover organizations that offer creative approaches to significantly raising the productivity of our investments in housing.

The economic benefit to taxpayers from recruiting volunteers to assist in the construction of new homes.

Habitat For Humanity

Home ownership has for many years been synonymous with "The American Dream." Habitat for Humanity helps families achieve and maintain home ownership in the core cities and inner-ring suburbs. The purchaser of a Habitat home benefits from the "sweat equity" donated by volunteers as well as from favorable first and second mortgage arrangements provided by the organization. Therefore, the impact and leverage achieved by the investor in Habitat are high. Purchasing families benefit from taking a significant step on the road to safety and self-sufficiency. The enhanced self image and stability of being a home owner positively impacts the performance of each family member. In addition to contributing to family stability, research on educational outcomes for children shows that kids of homeowners score higher on math and reading achievement tests and are less likely to have behavioral problems. Professionals in the field say that over a 25-year time frame savings to taxpayers could exceed $3,000 to $4,000 annually by investing in subsidized ownership versus subsidized rental housing. Ultimately Minnesota taxpayers and philanthropic investors benefit from programs that offer the high probability that social service support costs will decline and personal incomes and tax receipts will rise.

Using conservative assumptions, the original investment by the public sector in a Habitat home is more than recovered early in the second year following construction. Thereafter, the return is about 40% annually ($1.40 for each $1.00 invested) to the State of Minnesota and its taxpayers. The philanthropic investor in a "Habitat Home" will achieve break-even in the fifth year after construction and thereafter earn a return to the community of 20% annually ($1.20 for each $1.00 invested) for the life of the home.

MANAGEMENT

Susan Haigh has led Twin Cities Habitat for Humanity as CEO and president since 2005, overseeing an executive staff of 10 and helping it become one of the most successful Habitat affiliates in the nation. She lives in St Paul with her husband and four daughters. She brings an extensive background in community service to Twin Cities Habitat having served for ten years as a Ramsey County Commissioner and twelve years as a chief deputy county attorney. Haigh currently serves on the Minnesota Housing Commissioner's Resource Committee, the Minnesota Housing Partnership Board, Habitat for Humanity U.S. Council's Finance Committee and the Macalester College Board of Trustees. She has served on the boards of numerous civic organizations dealing with the issues of light rail, solid waste management, health care, public libraries and community development. Haigh holds a B.A. in Political Science from Macalester College and a J.D. from the William Mitchell College of Law.

Alan Raymond, senior vice president for programs & services is an architect with more than 30 years experience in construction, community development, real estate and land conservation. He oversaw land acquisition projects for the Trust for Public Land in the central USA region for 15 years prior to joining Habitat in 2005. He also served as president of Shelter Resources, Inc., an architecture and construction management company.

Robert White, vice president & chief financial officer, joined Habitat in 2001 and has been involved in affordable housing since 1982 as Vice President of Finance for the national home building and mortgage finance division of Insilco Corporation. His financial experience includes construction accounting, cash management, financial reporting, placing publicly traded mortgage-backed bonds, sale and pledging of mortgage notes.

Nancy Brady, vice president for resource development and community relations has over 15 years of non-profit leadership experience overseeing capital campaigns, corporate relations, donor cultivation and strategic marketing. Prior to moving to Minnesota in 2000 she spent ten years at the March of Dimes as the national director of strategic marketing. She is also a former team member of Greenwich Associates, a business strategy consulting firm in Connecticut.

The board of directors has 18 members including representatives of leading corporations such as General Mills, Ecolab, United Health

Group, Medica Health Partners, Minneapolis Federal Reserve Bank and Compass Airlines. The Northwest Area Foundation and Northway Community Trust are represented on the board as well as other business leaders and community activists.

ORGANIZATIONAL STRUCTURE

Twin Cities Habitat is organized with three operating divisions: Programs, Resource Development and Community Relations, and Finance and Support. Under the Programs Division are functions for construction, property management and family services. Resource development & community relations includes the areas of fund raising, marketing, government relations and advocacy and volunteer recruitment. Finance & support houses the critical functions of mortgage portfolio management, debt management, controller, human resources, technology and facilities management.

Homes are built and sold to families earning between 30% and 50% of the area median income at well below market prices. The average Habitat family income is $34,600. Purchasing families pay no more than 30% of their income annually. A typical Habitat family has 4 members headed by a single parent or with both parents working. They have often moved frequently between market-based rental and publicly subsidized housing and occupy overcrowded living spaces. Habitat homes include single-family homes, twin homes and multi-family homes. On average the direct cost to build a Twin Cities Habitat home is approximately $184,000. When fundraising and other overhead costs are included the average cost rises to $219,000. The typical Habitat home is 1,400 square feet with three bedrooms. Between 50-60 families move into Habitat homes each year. By March 2009, 750 families had purchased Habitat homes in the Twin Cities. Twin Cities Habitat for Humanity trains and engages over 20,000 volunteers each year. On any given day during peak construction periods more than 270 volunteers may be working on a single home.

Habitat homebuyers are working families including bank tellers, clergy members, retail clerks, security guards, tailors, food service workers, truck drivers, nurse's aids, taxi drivers, teacher's aids, factory workers, groundskeepers, custodians, housekeepers, medical technicians and parking attendants. Habitat homebuyers must complete 300-500 hours of sweat equity and attend 11 homebuyer classes including: money management, home safety, home maintenance and the requirements for being a good neighbor. Mortgage assistance to Habitat homeowners is generous, with a no-interest first mortgage provided on the construction cost of $184,000. A no-interest no-principal payment second mortgage is also provided when there is a difference between construction cost and market value. This is forgiven after 30 years. In response to the growing number of mortgage payment delinquencies in the Twin Cities, Habitat counsels homeowners with respect to delinquent payments on mortgages. In-depth counseling is provided to 110 clients annually with phone counseling to an additional 500 clients.

TESTIMONIAL

Living in subsidized housing with three small children and one income, Angie and Mike Wurm felt that the dream of home-ownership would never become a reality. A friend of the family told the Wurms about the homebuyer program at Twin Cities Habitat for Humanity (TCHFH). "We applied but didn't ever think we would get it. We felt like good things just didn't happen to us," said Angie. After three years of waiting, the call finally came, notifying them that they were matched to a house in Columbia Heights, Minnesota. "I will never forget that moment of joy and excitement when they called us and told us that we were getting a house," said Angie. A generous neighbor watched their children for free so that Angie could complete her sweat equity hours. "I worked on our house every single day from the day they started on it until the day we moved in. One Saturday I couldn't work, so I packed up a lunch and the kids and we sat across the street and watched," said Angie.

The couple was overwhelmed by the level of volunteer participation. "Over 400 volunteers took time out of their lives, took vacation time from their jobs, to work really hard on building a house for somebody they didn't even know. It was amazing to us that people were willing to do that," she said. After moving into their new home with the stability of a fixed mortgage payment, the couple began the work of building a better future for their family. Mike went back to school to further his education, which resulted in several promotions and salary increases. Angie started an in-home daycare and volunteered at TCHFH for five and one half years. The family finished the basement of their home, adding two bedrooms, a bathroom, family room and laundry. Eventually they sold the home and moved to Ham Lake, Minnesota. "We still drive by our Habitat house on our way to church. There are lots of good memories there," says Angie.

Calculating the Return on Investment

Conservative projections show a shortfall of 33,000 units of affordable housing for the state and 22,000 for the Twin City metropolitan area. The demographic profile for our future workforce needs show the state facing a shortage of skilled and semi-skilled workers over the next two decades. Therefore, attracting and holding a qualified workforce requires that attractive, safe and affordable housing be available. This will require the construction of both rental and owner-occupied affordable housing. Both will be in high demand as renters become homeowners replaced in turn by new immigrants to the state who become renters.

Therefore the addition of each new unit of affordable housing is likely to bring with it a new or upgraded worker who was a previous renter. This in turn frees a rental unit for a new worker. Thus each new unit of housing benefits from the economic contribution of the new family. This benefit takes the form of more tax revenue to the state and lower social service costs as families gain stability, avoid expensive emergency room care and other social service costs.

It costs about $219,000 on average to build a Habitat home including management and overhead expense. The state invests nearly $33,000 or 15% of the total. Home sales generate $78,000 of the cost or about 35% of the total. Philanthropy accounts for almost $88,000 of the cost or 40.0% with in kind services and other costs totaling $20,000 or 10%.

- *The state recovers its initial investment of $33,000 early in the second year following construction (taxes received related to construction of $13,567 in year one and the annual tax and "stability benefit" of the owner of $13,300 X 2). Thereafter the state receives a 40% ROI annually ($13,300/ $33,000) after having recovered all of its initial investment.*

- *The philanthropic investor will benefit in the first year after construction from taxes related to construction of $13,567 reducing their $88,000 initial investment to $66,637. Then for all years there is the economic benefit of creating a new home owner (stability benefit/real estate & sales taxes paid/free up of subsidized rental unit) of $13,300 It will then take the philanthropic investor an additional five years to recover their investment. By the sixth year after construction, the philanthropic investor will be providing an economic return of 20% annually to the community ($13,300/$66,637) on their investment.*

FACTS AND ASSUMPTIONS:

The direct cost to build a Habitat home is $184,000
The total cost including all Habitat overhead is $219,000
The average market value is $180,000
The buyer's annual income is on average $34,600
Annual real estate taxes are estimated at 1% of market value
The buyer is expected to pay an additional $1,000 in sales taxes annually
Stable housing will save government an estimated $3,000 annually in
  social service, better education outcomes, emergency medical and
  criminal justice system expense.
5% of Habitat new homeowners free up a subsidized rental unit for a
  new low income renter.

RETURN TO THE STATE AFTER COMPLETION OF ONE HOME

Sales Tax (6.5% on 40% of the construction cost)	$4,784
Income Tax Paid by contractors and workers	
(7.05% of 60% of the construction cost)	7,783
Mortgage Registry Tax (.0023% of the debt)	500
Deed Tax paid when deed recorded (.0033% of the value)	500
First Year Return to the State	$13,567

ECONOMIC CONTRIBUTION BY THE NEW HOME OWNER

Annual Real Estate Tax at 1% of $180,000 market value	$1,800
Increased Sales Taxes paid annually by owner	1,000
Value of low income rental home freed up by new home owner*	7,500
Stability Benefit of home ownership at 30% of income with	
no interest versus rental at nearly 50% of annual income**	3,000
Total Annual Contribution by Owner	$13,300

*The assumption here is that 5% of new Habitat homeowners free up a subsidized rental unit that would have been built at a cost of $150,000. **Stability benefit derived from the estimated high cost of medical and social service support for highly mobile low income families, enhanced education outcomes for children and improved climate for job stability. Not included are Payroll Taxes paid annually by the new homeowner's employer ($2,000) if he/she is a net new addition to the workforce.

CRITIQUE

Habitat management has to estimate the percentage of its new home-owners who free up a subsidized rental unit, estimated to cost $150,000. The calculation above is believed conservative and assumes that 5% of new homeowners do in fact free up a subsidized unit for another family. Management believes the actual number is closer to 15%, which, if true, dramatically increases the returns for both government and philanthropic investors. Follow-up studies to track these patterns of residential occupancy would be advantageous to philanthropy and government at all levels. The stability benefit estimate is also supported by the fact that studies show a savings to taxpayers over time for subsidized home ownership versus subsidized rental housing. Longitudinal studies that better document these assumptions would obviously be helpful.

Common Bond Communities

Common Bond Communities has pioneered the concept of "afford-able housing linked to services" with remarkable success. This analysis explores the added return on investment derived when a range of support services are effectively located on the premises of affordable housing sites. Common Bond Communities is Minnesota's largest non-profit provider of affordable housing, serving nearly 8,000 residents in over 5,000 affordable apartments and townhomes. Residents reside in 42 facilities located in 107 urban and suburban housing communities and small cities in the region. The annual budget of about $14 million is nearly 67% funded by earned income. Historically affordable housing providers have been in the bricks and mortar business, constructing and managing rental properties. Experience has shown that housing must be effectively linked with human services if low-income people with special needs are to have the resources to become self-reliant.

The July 2006 study conducted by Common Bond Communities Public Policy Task Force, comprised of seven Twin Cities civic leaders, concluded that for every dollar invested in Common Bond's "Seven Key Affordable Housing Services" the public received a 64% return on investment over a one year time frame ($1.64 received for each $1.00 invested).

In a different study, namely a field test involving 56 housing sites in 34 cities serving low-income clients over a one year period, Common Bond found that every dollar invested in a "housing with services" program resulted in at least $1.55 in social value or a one year return on investment of 55%.

PROGRAM OVERVIEW

The Advantage Center service delivery model within Common Bond is more than 16 years old, delivering services to senior citizens, many of whom are at risk; working-age head of households, of whom many are single mothers, and low income children. Among these clients are increasing numbers of working poor, people with mental and physical challenges, and refugees and immigrants. The overall goals are to help heads of households find and hold jobs with benefits, so that they can move on to market rate rental or home ownership; insure that school-age children have a regular adult role model so that they can achieve their highest academic potential, and finally to train senior citizens to live independently in their own homes. Core programs include: "Career Advantage" which assists residents in finding and keeping living-wage jobs with benefits; "Study Buddies" where consistent one-on-one mentoring for at-risk youth aims to enhance academic achievement; "Customized Services Coordination" which stabilizes families by increasing access to community-based educational and service resources; Computer Labs which help close the "digital divide" between rich and poor and "Community Boards and Resident Associations" that enrich lives, generating a sense of ownership along with leadership, volunteer service and recreational opportunities.

MANAGEMENT

Paul Fate is president and CEO of Common Bond. He succeeded Joe Errigo who founded the organization in 1981 and retired in 2006. Mr. Fate has over 25 years of experience in the field of housing and community development. Previously he was executive director of Payne Lake Community Partners, a community development initiative hosted by the Minneapolis-based McKnight Foundation and affiliated with a consortium of national funders, financial institutions and federal departments known as "Living Cities". He started and directed the Minneapolis office of LISC (Local Initiatives Support Organization) raising and investing over $110 million which resulted in more than 3,000 units of affordable housing built and nearly $500 million in housing and economic development in Twin Cities neighborhoods. He holds a master's degree in public administration from Harvard University and master's degree in city planning from the University of Minnesota.

Executive positions include the chief operating officer who oversees managers for business development, housing development, property management, administration, human resources and information services) and vice presidents for resource development and Advantage Center Services (seniors /special needs/family programs/AmeriCorps programs/government grants). Management has made extensive use of volunteers to assist with financial development and program support. In 2009 over 1,900 volunteers were utilized coming from leading corporations such as Target, Comcast, General Electric, Wells Fargo, 3M, Cummins Power Generation, Ernst & Young, Goodrich Corporation, Opus, BBDO, Frito Lay, McKesson Corporation and several church based, educational and civic organizations. The board of directors is comprised of nine community leaders with professional experience in housing, public finance, banking, community development and metropolitan governance.

Testimonial

Amrula is a political refugee from Ethiopia who says, "It takes time to be accepted in a new society." At first he struggled to find a steady job and learn how to fit into American culture. In Common Bond's Skyline Tower he found stability for his family in a safe environment. As his family grew he found support in Common Bond's Career Advantage program which helped him build his resume and get training that prepared him for the world of work. Next came help securing a scholarship for the Emerge City Skills maintenance training program. He completed the training in six weeks while at the same time driving a taxi, and was offered a job at Seward Towers in Minneapolis. His family is now thriving, and his eldest daughter just received several academic excellence awards. Amrula concludes saying about his four children, "They have good access to schools and they are lucky to be here!"

Calculating the Advantage Center Cost Savings

Separate calculations have been made for each of the seven categories of Advantage Center support services.

– Welfare Reform

The annual savings to the MFIP system amount to $32,829 (93 individuals placed in jobs decreasing MFIP payments $353 each). HUD housing subsidy savings totaled $30,718 per year (93 people placed in jobs with an increase in earnings of $1,101 each) or a total of $102,393 which multiplied by the 30% rule saves HUD $30,718 per year. This same wage gain of $102,393 at an 11% overall tax bracket adds $11,263 to the government's tax base. With an annual job retention rate of 74% an additional savings of $55,359 is realized from the previous year's clients served.

— Mental Health
Publicly subsidized health costs saved amounted to $117,600 (24 health emergencies prevented at an average cost for three days in a psychiatric ward of $4,900). Case management costs avoided by the public system totaled $12,672 (576 hours of case management avoided at an average hourly cost of $22).

— Homelessness Prevention
30-day shelter costs avoided totaled $416,500 per year (85 shelter stays avoided at a per 30 day cost of $4,900). HUD unit turnover costs avoided were $231,080 (424 evictions prevented at an average HUD cost of $545 per eviction).

— Child Protection
Foster Care Savings were $235,440 (18 out of home 18 month placements avoided costing $13,080 each). Case management savings were $156,960 (18 out of home placements avoided where case management cost for 18 months would have totaled $8,720 each).

— Crime Prevention
A modest uptick in crime during the period caused an uptick in crime related expenses (police calls, arrest and incarceration) of $8,943.

— School Achievement
149 children paired with mentors avoided the need for a Title 1 instructor and saved the school system $36,190. 100% of these advanced to the next grade level saving the schools $35,136 in remedial instruction. 15,496 hours of after-school care was provided and assuming 20% of parents would have chosen state-subsidized child care as an alternative (at $22/hour) state child care savings of $68,182 were realized.

— Long Term Care Reform
518 senior residents needed 3 or more services that would on average have required at least 130 nursing home placements for an average of 6 months each. At an average cost of $3,270 per month total savings amounted to $2,540,790.

Calculating the Return on Investment from Advantage Center Services

TOTAL SAVINGS

Welfare Reform	$32,829	MFIP
	$30,718	HUD
	$11,263	tax base
	$55,359	job retention
Mental Health	$117,600	avoid emergency services
	$12,672	case management savings
Homelessness Prevention	$416,500	shelter costs avoided
	$231,080	avoid HUD turnover costs
Child Protection	$235,440	foster care savings
	$156,960	case management savings
Crime Prevention	(9,628)	crime prevention costs
School Achievement	$36,190	reduced need for TITLE 1
	$35,136	save on remedial program
Child Care	$68,182	state child care savings
Long-term Care Reform	$2,540,790	avoided nursing home costs

TOTAL PROGRAM SAVINGS	$3,971,091
TOTAL PROGRAM COSTS	$2,416,448
NET BENEFIT	$1,554,643

ROI CALCULATIONS

• On an absolute basis and ignoring the impact of leverage, the total return on investment for Common Bond Communities Advantage Center services over a period of one year amounts to 64% ($1,554,643 /$2,416,448).

• Because the private sector (individuals/foundations/in kind contributions) contributes only 40% of the total Common Bond budget, the return to the philanthropic community is more than twice as high as stated above. More than 50% of their funding comes from fee income, interest income and other sources.

• The public investment is less than 10% resulting in an even higher return to taxpayers from a relatively small investment by government.

CRITIQUE

The Common Bond analysis despite its complexity, demonstrates that it is possible to set up an accounting system that calculates the value added from a range of quite different but critical family support services. It reminds one of the pioneering work done in the early design of industrial cost accounting systems. The cost data was prepared by the Common Bond Communities Public Policy Task Force comprised of five independent civic leaders and two Common Bond Board members experienced in low income housing programs. Once again, a longitudinal study would help verify the savings in all areas, with particular attention to savings from delaying entrance into expensive long-term care. Common Bond's gift to the affordable housing scene is the clear benefit of adding quality support services that meet the needs of the full range of family ages.

Community Land Trusts reduce the cost to government of providing affordable workforce housing to lower-income workers

City of Lakes Land Trust

The formation of Community Land Trusts is accelerating nationally as a vehicle to make home ownership affordable to low and moderate income families. The concept involves freezing, to the extent possible, a significant portion of the increases in the cost of home ownership over a very long period of time. Historically the gap continues to widen between the cost of housing and wages earned by the average household. When families pay more than 30% of their income for housing, the family is stressed financially and moves frequently seeking affordable rent; this, in turn, impacts school performance, job performance, child care costs and transportation logistics. Substandard housing impacts family health, results in overcrowding and often increases the chances of criminal justice system involvement.

The benefits from Community Land Trusts (CLTs) are many. The purchasing family frees up an affordable rental unit and benefits from becoming home owners, thereby establishing equity in their home. The family can now anticipate a growing equity base that enhances their credit rating and permits eventual ownership of a market rate home. Taxpayers benefit from the stability home ownership brings to the family, which, in turn, keeps the children in the same school longer, permits home owners to focus on their employment career more effectively and reduces the social costs related to families constantly on the move seeking affordable, safe and often subsidized rental housing. Interestingly, the 2009 foreclosure rate on CLTs was well below that of comparable market rate homes. In fact a survey by a researcher at Vanderbilt University concluded that conventional home owners were 8 times more likely to be in the process of foreclosure than CLT homeowners at the end of the 4th quarter of 2009.

The City of Lakes Community Land Trust (CLCLT), which serves Minneapolis residents, evolved from a collaboration of Powderhorn Residents Group (PRG), Seward Redesign, Powderhorn Park Neighborhood

Association (PPNA) and Lyndale Neighborhood Development Corporation (LNDC) that began in late 2001. CLCLT provides permanently affordable housing for low to moderate income home buyers by owning the land, but selling the home on the land to an income-qualified buyer. It does this by bringing an affordable investment, typically ranging from 20% to 50% of the total property cost, to assist the homeowner in the purchase. The CLCLT then assigns this affordability investment to the title of the land to ensure the home will remain perpetually affordable. The home owner then leases the land through a renewable ground lease. When the homeowner sells the house their equity plus 25% of the appreciated value is returned to them, and 75% of the appreciated value remains with CLCLT to make the same home affordable to future buyers. Over 170,000 low income Twin Cities metropolitan area households are currently paying more than they can afford (30% of their income is the industry standard) for housing. Many of these are renters who are not building equity through home ownership. In addition, an estimated 22,000 households lack affordable housing in the Twin Cities Metropolitan Area. While 35% of Minneapolis residents are people of color only 15% are "communities of color" home owners.

Based on forty-eight months' experience, and drawing upon the experience of other land trusts, dollars invested by CLCLT as of December 2008 provided a return to CLCLT, after recovery of their original investment, of 105% over a ten-year time frame, and 270% over a twenty-year time frame ($3.70 for each $1.00 invested).

One of the best measures of the productivity of dollars invested by CLCLT is the fact that between 130 to 160 new home owners would have been created over these respective time periods. The community investors in CLCLT are a combination of private and public organizations.

MANAGEMENT

Jeff Washburne has served as executive director of the City of Lakes Community Land Trust since November of 2002. He previously worked at Twin City Neighborhood Housing Services from 1997 to 2002 serving as executive director the last two years. Prior to his nonprofit housing experience, Washburne worked as a construction supervisor and trainer for a residential construction firm in South Korea, a YMCA program manager in New Mexico, and served as a Peace Corps volunteer in Honduras. He holds a M.A. in Public Administration from Hamline University and a B.A. in Psychology from DePauw University. He currently serves on several community boards including The Minneapolis Consortium of Community Developers and the Minnesota Land Trust Coalition. Project director Staci Horwitz, outreach coordinator Barbara Lightsy and communications manager Carrie Christensen have had distinguished careers in public service prior to joining CLCLT. The fifteen-member board of directors includes leaders from corporations such as Wells Fargo and Center Point Energy as well as Allina Health Systems, University of Minnesota, City of Minneapolis and a number of leading community based organizations and members well versed in real estate development.

ORGANIZATIONAL STRUCTURE

The staff of four includes the executive director, project director, outreach coordinator and communications manager. Fundraising and community relations are key responsibilities for the executive director in addition to managing the finances and general oversight responsibilities. The project director oversees the buyer education and qualification process as well as homebuyer initiated transactions. The outreach coordinator is the lead liaison with CLCLT homeowners. The communications manager communicates with neighborhood organizations to identify prospective new homeowners and available properties, and also works to create greater awareness of CLCLT in the community. A typical CLCLT family has 2.5 members, 56% headed by a single mother, is a first time buyer, has an average income of $32,000 and is comprised of 46% people of color with 14% new Americans.

CLCLT homes on average have had a market value of approximately $174,000 and sell for about $120,000 requiring a subsidy or non-owner investment of $54,000. The sources for the non-owner investment include: Minnesota Housing Finance Agency, the Family Housing Fund, Hennepin County, The City of Minneapolis and others including neighborhood groups and family/corporate foundations. From September 2004 to December 2008 eighty four homes were sold to qualified buyers. By December 2009 a total of 101 homes were sold. In 2007 and 2008 CLCLT began to see some of the first re-sales of their homes, permitting original owners to move on to other now affordable market rate homes and freeing up opportunity for new first time home owners. National experience shows that CLCLT type homes resell between five and ten years after purchase.

Testimonial

One of the first CLCLT homebuyers was a single mother with two young children who had been pursuing home ownership for numerous years. Living in the Lyndale neighborhood of South Minneapolis and working as a proof writer, she had become discouraged over the cost of housing and/or the amount of rehab required on more affordable home-ownership in South Minneapolis. At that time, the neighborhood association had agreed to grant $90,000 of their housing funding to CLCLT. The prospective homebuyer learned about the opportunity to purchase a home of her choice through a neighborhood newspaper. She was pre-approved for a $120,000 loan and was qualified for $65,000 in affordability assistance from CLCLT. When she came up on the wait list she and her realtor found a home to purchase listed at $185,000. CLCLT ordered an inspection, the home passed and they signed a purchase agreement. Prior to the closing in the summer of 2006 she met with an attorney, paid for by CLCLT, who reviewed all the documents. She had purchased a home for $120,000 and was entitled to her equity invested, plus 25% of the appreciated value if she later decides to sell the home. Her two children attend the same neighborhood school as before and she is actively involved in the community.

Calculating the Return on Investment

Based on the $4,257,000 investment by CLCLT (philanthropic investors and neighborhood organizations) as of December 31, 2008, the total gain in appreciated value of the 84 homes purchased with a total value of $13,700,000 was about $447,000, reflecting the dramatic decline in home values in 2008. For purposes of estimating future annual gains in value, a conservative figure of 2.5% was used. The average value of homes purchased was $174,000 and the price paid by homeowners $120,000, requiring an investment of $54,000 by CLCLT. Assuming on average 2.5% appreciation in future years the average annual gain in value per unit would be $4,350. Since CLCLT recaptures 75% of this gain, they add about $274,000 to their equity base each year from the 84 existing units. It is assumed that when a home resells, the appreciation benefit to MCLCT (75%) continues with the new owner. In other words, over a twenty year period MCLCT recaptures $5,480,000 (Condos and Single Family Homes). These are dollars that represent savings to investors and taxpayers in future years.

The other assumed benefits to taxpayers and investors include real estate taxes paid (assume 1% of market), an estimate of the economic benefits of moving a renter to home-owner status (family stability, education gains for children, and equity build up), and finally the fact that a rental unit has been freed up for another low income family. These last two assumptions are best guesses, but believed to be conservative. Studies have documented the value of home ownership over rental at greater values than used here. Also, if less than 2% of CLCLT homeowners come from subsidized rental units the $2,000 would be a realistic best guess (2% of $175,000 cost to build a new rental unit is $3,500). Because these three added benefits continue with the homeowners in future years they multiply over time depending on the assumed turnover rate. Assuming a ten year turnover rate for single homes, 76 new home owners are created over twenty years. Assuming a five year turnover rate for condominiums, 184 new home owners could be created over a twenty year time frame. The program is designed for long term impact and therefore long time periods to calculate productivity and return on investment are appropriate.

FACTS & ASSUMPTIONS: 12/31/08

Initial Investment by CLCLT: $4,257,996
Number of Homes (55% Condominiums & 45% Single Homes): 84
Average Market Sales Price (2004-2008): $174,000
Average CLCLT Affordability Gap Investment: $54,000
Average Real Estate Taxes Paid: $2,000
Homeowner Economic Contribution (Stability Benefit): $2,000
Assume annual gain in value at 2.5%: $4,350
CLCLT Share of Annual Appreciation: 75%
Turnover Rate for Condominiums: 5 Years
Turnover Rate for Single Homes: 10 Years
Discount Rate for Present Value Analysis: 5.00%

Returns for Condos	Unit	Units	10 years	20 years
CLCLT 75% Equity Gain	$3,260	$150,000	$1,500,000	$3,000,000
Real Estate Taxes Paid	2,000	92,000	1,380,000	4,600,000
Homeowner Economic Contribution	2,000	92,000	1,380,000	4,600,000
Freeing Up a Subsidized Rental Unit	2,000	92,000	1,380,000	4,600,000
Total	$9,260	$426,000	$3,520,000	$16,800,000
New Homeowners (5 Year Turnover Rate)			92	184

Returns for Single Homes	Unit	Units	10 years	20 years
CLCLT 75% Equity Gain	$3,260	$124,000	$1,240,000	$2,480,000
Real Estate Taxes Paid	2,000	76,000	760,000	1,520,000
Homeowner Economic Contribution	2,000	76,000	760,000	1,520,000
Freeing Up a Subsidized Rental Unit	2,000	76,000	760,000	1,520,000
Total	$9,260	$352,000	$5,640,000	$7,040,000
New Homeowners (10 Year Turnover Rate)			38	76

Total for Condominiums & Single Homes $9,160,000 $23,840,000

Present Value @ 5.00%, (Net 2.5%) * $8,732,000 $15,734,000
Initial Investment by CLCLT $4,258,000
Total Return 105% 270%

*The Equity Gain, Real Estate Taxes Paid, Homeowner Economic Contribution and Freeing up a Subsidized Rental Unit values have not been inflated at 2.5% for the future time periods (to keep the math simple). Therefore, the Present Value has been computed at 2.5% rather than 5.00%, a rate which would be closer to long term mortgage rates. Also the numbers do not reflect the recently reported additional seventeen homes sold in 2009.

CRITIQUE

Much work remains to be done to accurately measure the economic benefit to taxpayers from the development and growth of community land trusts. However, even conservative assumptions show that the returns can be favorable assuming investors have a ten year time horizon or greater. State housing authorities would do well to track the true savings in housing land costs over extended periods of time including both periods of rising and declining land value. Given historic trends in land values, I believe that the returns calculated above are likely understated.

Housing, educating and preparing single mothers
for the world of work

The Jeremiah Program

Major metropolitan areas continue to have a shortage of shelters for chronically homeless families. Where shelter is available, only a few providers offer the supportive services that move families out of poverty and into self-sufficiency. When single men and women move frequently to obtain shelter, their potential to enter and/or remain in the workforce is limited. In the case of single mothers, longer-term effective rehabilitative support will not be available if a social worker has no way of locating the family. The chronically homeless incur a host of public sector intervention costs including: out of home placement, chemical dependency treatment, criminal justice system encounters, emergency room service and AFDC and state welfare support. The initial expense involved with well-managed housing programs having quality supportive services is high. However, the longer term payoff to taxpayers from programs like The Jeremiah Program in the Twin Cities remains one of the region's best kept secrets!

The Jeremiah Program was launched in 1998 by the Rev. Michael O'Connell with the acceptance of 18 families into residence. Its mission is "to transform families from poverty to prosperity." Jeremiah is a leading innovator in providing supportive services to chronically homeless single mothers and their children. Experience shows that these services not only substantially reduce the longer-term cost to society of caring for these families, but also produce adults prepared for the world of work and children ready to learn. There are significant costs to taxpayers incurred by homeless families who do not have access to supportive housing.

The enrollees' journey to self-reliance begins with what Jeremiah calls "Foundational Support," which calls for safe and secure housing, quality early childhood education and a sustainable/supportive community. Building upon that base are programs for "Skill and Vision Building," which involves empowerment experiences, job skills and life skills. This then sets the stage for "Post Secondary Education" which in turn opens the door for "Gainful Employment Toward a Career."

Comparing Jeremiah's costs for over 30 months of support to 77 families with the longer-term reduction in public service intervention costs highlighted in the Family Housing Fund report, it appears that break-even is exceeded three years after the single mother's graduation. By the fourth year, the return on investment for the community exceeds 50% ($1.50 returned for every $1.00 invested). This includes taxes paid by the mother due to her placement in jobs earning on average $14.77 per hour after graduation.

MANAGEMENT

Gloria Perez has been president and CEO of Jeremiah Program since its founding in 1998. She had previously served as executive director of Casa de Esperanza, a local domestic violence agency in St. Paul, Minnesota. She brings more than 19 years of management, supervision and leadership experience to her position. She also possesses experience in administrative-level fundraising, strategic planning and organizational best practices as a board member for several community and non-profit organizations. In addition she has management and customer service experience in the insurance and restaurant industries.

Gloria is a native of San Antonio, Texas, and applies her rich Latina cultural background to her work as an advocate for women, families and people of color. She is the youngest of three girls raised by their mother after the death of their father at an early age, and was the first college graduate in her family, having completed her degree at Macalester College. She serves on the boards of leading community organizations in the fields of health care, housing, higher education and philanthropy. She is the recipient of numerous civic awards including the Ellis Island Medal of Honor. Gloria Perez lives in St. Paul with her two children.

The board of directors is comprised of 35 leaders from business, government, philanthropy, the legal profession, non-profit organizations and the community at large. Major corporations represented include Target, Wells Fargo, Xcel Energy, Bank of America, Cargill, US Bank, 3M, Ernst & Young and Ameriprise Financial.

ORGANIZATIONAL STRUCTURE

With facilities in both Minneapolis and St Paul Jeremiah operates with a staff of 40. Key operating functions include directors of early childhood education, adult education & employment, strategic partnerships & volunteerism and admissions & alumni relations. Early childhood education is the largest division including 16 child care teachers in Minneapolis and St. Paul. Life skills coaches who work with the single mothers are housed at both locations. Other key functions are headed by directors of advancement and finance/administration.

The program serves low-income single mothers with children who are under age five at the time of application. Families come from unstable housing with 30% coming from homeless shelters. Mothers are at least eighteen years of age, must have a high-school diploma or GED and be accepted to or enrolled in a vocational or other post-secondary training program. Children are enrolled in the on- site Child Development Center where they engage in social, emotional, intellectual and physical development activities. Classrooms house children ages infant to five. Seventy-seven families are housed at the two locations. Jeremiah partners with educational institutions, non-profit organizations, congregations, corporations and a number of community groups for specific services that support resident families.

Women enter the program earning on average $8.39 an hour and graduate on average within two and one half years earning $15.39 an hour. Many have relied upon public assistance and have not paid taxes. Part of the curriculum is learning how to manage debt and practice good financial management. Graduates earn at a minimum an Associate of Arts degree and 30% earn a four year degree. Graduates are able to afford safe housing and 20% are homeowners. Many of the children come from difficult poverty experiences. Graduates who were willing to share information report that their children are now performing at age appropriate developmental levels.

TESTIMONIAL

When Meeze came to Jeremiah she was four months pregnant. "I told my child's father, 'We are both going to college and we are living in student housing,'" she recalls. "We didn't know what to do. We were confused and wondering, where do we go from here?"

Then Meeze saw an announcement about the Jeremiah Program and how it serves single moms going to college. "I thought, that sounds like me!" she says. "It was perfect." During the admission process she was helped by her life skills coach Rebecca Magner. "She was so sweet and everyone here seemed so happy. And with daycare downstairs—you can't beat that." Meeze's daughter, Raquel, started at the Child Development Center when she was six weeks old. "She loves the center and has bonded with the other children and the teachers," says Meeze. She describes the teachers as "very flexible and compassionate."

Learning parenting skills has been helpful to both mother and child. "I got a lot of ideas from those classes," Meeze states. "After I pick up Raquel from daycare, I always try to spend an hour playing with her, listening to music, trying to stimulate her. I want her to know that she is lovable, important and valuable. I try to live that, myself, everyday, so that she sees me living it." Raquel also benefits from a close relationship with her father, a University of Minnesota student.

Meeze will complete her medical assistant course at Everest Institute in October. Then using a $1,500 scholarship recently awarded to her by the Executive Women International and Women Venture, she will finish her associate degree at Minneapolis Community and Technical College. After that, she hopes to enter a training program offered at the Minneapolis VA Hospital. "The VA will actually pay me while I'm learning to be a radiology technician," Meeze says. The two-year program runs five days a week from 7 a.m. until 5 p.m. and pays $14 an hour to start. (She currently earns $9.25 an hour working part time at Victoria's Secret.)

The Family Housing Fund study of 2002 tracked a single mother with three young children over a nine-year period. This mother dropped out of school at age 14 because of her addiction to crack cocaine. She could not maintain recovery in treatment, required her foster mother to care for her children, served jail time for drug possession and prostitution and eventually entered a supportive housing community. At this facility she designed a self- sufficiency plan that eventually helped her achieve a more stable life.

CALCULATING THE JEREMIAH PROGRAM'S COST SAVINGS

The analysis begins by adjusting the Family Housing Fund model to attain comparability with the average family served by The Jeremiah Program. Rather than the family of four used in the FHF study, Jeremiah's average family includes a single mother with one and one half children.

Cost Comparisons With And Without Supportive Housing*

Public Service Intervention Costs	Cost Without Supportive Housing	Cost With Supportive Housing
Out of Home Placement for Children	$99,700	$ 0
Chemical Dependency Treatment Support	9,000	39,200
Criminal Justice	48,800	0
Hospital/Medical	281,200	38,200
Housing	6,000	52,400
AFDC/MFIP	69,100	69,100
Case Management	54,500	24,200
Child Care	77,500	85,200
Employment	200	2,600
Academic Development	48,600	5,900
Transportation	0	12,700
Total (Nine Years)	$695,200	$337,100
Total (Annual Average)	$77,200	$37,500

Adjusting the FHF study to reflect the smaller family size reduces the FHF average annual cost without supportive services to $44,500 or 57.6% of the original figure of $77,200. Jeremiah's per family operating cost for 2009 was $46,700 (total budget of $3.6 Million divided by seventy seven families).

To move families to self-sufficiency, Jeremiah provides a safe living environment, advanced day care and child development facilities, access to employment and education, and comprehensive life skills education (job seeking and retention skills, communication skills, self-esteem and emotion control, parenting and child development skills, financial responsibility, healthy relationships and sexuality and general health and wellness). Training can be individualized as the program evolves over the thirty months to graduation.

The financial analysis extends the cost assumptions for a family without supportive housing over nine years as reflected in the FHF study. In addition Jeremiah graduates earn on average $14.77 per hour which generate conservatively $2,000 per year in Minnesota tax revenue. Finally, since 15% of revenues are public funds, 70% philanthropic contributions, 14% earned income and 1% other income, there is a leveraging impact that benefits both the private contributor and the tax payer.

- *With a total investment of $116,750 per family (over 30 months) The Jeremiah Program can more than recover its costs three years after graduation ($133,500/$116,750) and provide the community with a better than 50% return on investment four years after graduation ($178,000/$116,750).*

- *Minnesota taxpayers (state and federal tax returns) provide only 15% of Jeremiah revenues. This leverage permits them to provide the community with break-even status early in the first year following graduation and better than a 150% return by year end ($44,500/$17,500).*

- *The philanthropic investor providing 70% of revenues to Jeremiah can exceed break-even status for the community two years following graduation ($89,000/$81,725) and gain a better than 100% return four years after graduation ($178,000/$81,725).*

The returns would be even higher if the per graduate economic benefit to Minnesota of an additional productive worker, and the multiplier effect of additional annual spending of $30,000 per graduate (earning $14.77/ hour) were included.

CALCULATING THE RETURN ON INVESTMENT*

	Year 1	Year 2	Year 3	Year 4	Year 5	Total to Year 9
No Supportive Housing FHF Study Public Costs	$44,500	$44,500	$44,500	$44,500	$44,500	$400,500
Jeremiah Private Costs	(No costs incurred following graduation after the initial investment of $116,750 over thirty months)					
Minnesota Taxes Paid	2,000	2,000	2,000	2,000	2,000	18,000
Jeremiah Program System Benefit	$46,500	$46,500	$46,500	$46,500	$46,500	$418,500

*Year one commences six months after completion of the thirty month program. The above numbers have not been adjusted to reflect their present value. It is assumed that a discount rate reflecting the relatively low level of interest rates would be offset by inflation. All numbers reflect their value in the year 2002 when the Family Housing Fund Study was completed. Family Housing Fund; Midwest Plaza West, Suite 1825, 801 Nicollet Mall, Minneapolis, MN 55402; Tel 612-375-9644.

CRITIQUE

The Jeremiah Program analysis requires that assumptions be made about what social service expenses would have been incurred had supportive housing not been available to a family. Fortunately for this study, the Minneapolis-based Twin Cities Family Housing Fund completed a detailed nine-year study in 2002 which lists the range of public intervention costs by sector for a chronically homeless family. One might question whether the per family ongoing costs cited in the Family Housing Fund study (even after adjusting for the reduced size of the average Jeremiah family) are appropriate and provide a fair comparison. However, the positive returns calculated remain extremely high, even if the public sector cost savings estimates are reduced by as much as 50%.

Preventing and/or delaying admission to
expensive nursing home care

Lifetrack Resources

L ifetrack Resources has been a leader in providing lifelong support to disadvantaged Minnesotans for more than 60 years. Lifetrack Resources serves over 10,000 individuals each year with an annual budget of over $10 million, ranking it as one of Minnesota's largest providers of family support services. The two main focus areas are Children & Healthy Family Development and Employment & Economic Opportunity. Lifetrack annually assists more than 650 young children who have been abused or neglected including their siblings and caregivers with therapeutic preschool and home visiting programs. Nearly all children enrolled demonstrate advancement in one or more developmental areas. Lifetrack is also a leading provider of speech, physical, occupational therapies and deaf and hard of hearing services for at risk children and adults.

Lifetrack resources for many years was the premier regional provider of services that assisted senior citizens to remain in their homes and delay entrance into nursing care facilities. This program's success was well documented by an independent study conducted by Public/Private Ventures and funded by the Annie E. Casey Foundation. Cutbacks in expenditures on the Medicare home health benefit, based on a somewhat controversial study by the Medicare Payment Advisory Commission in the late 1970s, forced the scale back and eventual termination of this program, viewed by many as one of the most cost-effective programs benefitting taxpayers. Nearly 2 million elderly Americans are being warehoused in nursing homes. Many of these with proper training could live independently or in many cases be reconnected with their families.

By comparing the cost of services Lifetrack provided to keep nursing home candidates in their own home ($7,600) with the average annual cost of nursing home care ($57,000) in Minnesota, one can conservatively conclude that Minnesota taxpayers more than *recouped their investment in six months, and earned a return on investment exceeding 100% ($2.00 returned for each $1.00 invested) eleven months after training was completed.*

MANAGEMENT

Trixie Ann Golberg is president and CEO of Lifetrack Resources, having joined the organization in 2006 following a successful career as president of the Southern Minnesota Initiative Foundation. In that capacity she transformed the organization into one that made a real difference in the lives of people and communities. Increased regional impact was achieved by expanding fundraising and programs that included community redesign, economic development and enhanced communications. She is well versed in strategic planning and the techniques of team building. She served as assistant director of programs at the Northwest Municipal Conference based in Des Plaines, Illinois from 1988 to 1993. Under her leadership this 40 member regional council of local governments helped guide precedent-setting negotiations on municipal/utility franchise agreements. Golberg has served on the boards of the Minnesota Council on Foundations, Rochester Area University Center, Owatonna College and University Center and currently is on the Ramsey County Workforce Investment Board and the Dakota County Human Service Advisory Board. She is also a University of Minnesota Humphrey Institute Fellow and Salzburg Policy Fellow.

ORGANIZATIONAL STRUCTURE

Lifetrack's therapeutic services allow people to stay safely and independently in their own homes for an extended period of time. With assistive devices and professional training, clients can learn to cook safely, eat efficiently, avoid falling, exercise, get dressed, use toilet facilities, entertain themselves and remain alert cognitively. On average, appropriate training and therapy may require anywhere from five to twenty visits by a trained professional over a one to two month period of time. Candidates for service may have been in a nursing home, convalescent care center, extended care facility or inpatient rehab facility. They might have been on a waiting list for a nursing home, considering admission to a nursing home, requiring or receiving constant supervision, receiving home health aide or nursing services a minimum of two times a week, or having a daily attendant.

During the years the program operated, Lifetrack typically helped 140 senior citizens avoid nursing home care in a given year. At an average daily rate of $126.50 nursing home costs in excess of $1.0 million were avoided. Through physical, occupational and speech-language therapy, the client builds endurance and compensatory skills to maintain their ability to achieve functional independence. Medical social workers assist with adjustment to disability, finances, housing and short term mental health needs. Lifetrack Resources has been recognized by the Minnesota Department of Health as an "Essential Community Provider," because of their effectiveness in integrating their stabilizing therapy services with medical services for persons who are uninsured, at high risk or have special needs.

TESTIMONIAL

The Jay and Rose Phillips family Foundation sponsored a follow-up study in 2006 that provided unique data on the success of this program. The study entitled "Adult Home Care Therapies Follow-Up Study" tracked 240 Lifetrack clients 12 months after their discharge and found that: 94% were still living at home, 77% maintained or improved their physical condition, 80% maintained or improved their mobility, 85% maintained or improved their ADLs (activities of daily living), 76% accessed community resources with 32% expressing issues or concerns. Of the 240 clients still living at home their total number of months not in nursing care was 1,677 translating into 140 years. The study concluded that for these 240 clients potential taxpayer savings (cost of 140 nursing care years less program cost) amounted to $6.9 million! A minimum of 29% of Lifetrack clients were on Medical Assistance resulting in confirmed taxpayer savings of $2.1 million.

The Phillips Family Foundation study recommended that: 1) Organizations like Lifetrack should continue to provide home healthcare services. 2) These organizations should advocate with governmental officials for increased funding for Home Care since current Medical Assistance reimbursements covers about 50% of the true cost of homecare in Minnesota (far less than in surrounding states. 3) Consider providing longer duration of rehabilitation therapies with less frequency as clients progress toward discharge. 4) Refer clients for occupational therapy to treat psychological and cognitive problem solving. 5) Continue with home care nurses, therapists and social workers referring clients to appropriate community resources within the initial 60 days of service.

Calculating the Return on Investment

Lifetrack experience is that therapy and training with independent living devices can require from five to twenty homecare visits over a two-month period. Complications such as medical problems (kidney disease, diabetes), unsafe housing, lack of family support, chemical dependency, mental illness and language issues may require additional therapy. This 60-day period is referred to as "an episode of care." Lifetrack's 2005 direct cost for an episode of care amounted to about $5,000, excluding assisted living devices, which are donated. Lifetrack partners with others for medical training and support. The medical support adds an additional $2,600 per episode of care to the total cost. The total investment for 60 days of client training and medical assistance is estimated to be about $7,600, or $127.00 per day.

In 2005, 351 individuals were determined to be "at risk" for institutional care. Of those who received Lifetrack support, 90% or 316 remained in their homes for at least sixty days after support was given and thereafter 120 for 57 days after support was initiated. Because there is as yet no effective way to measure relative performance through such techniques as the use of control groups, it is not certain that all who received in-home care avoided institutionalization because of Lifetrack support. To be conservative, an assumed avoidance rate of 50% has been used to determine the rate of return to Minnesota taxpayers.

While the average cost for one year of nursing home care was approximately $56,922 in 2005 it is likely that taxpayers did not bear the full brunt of this expense. The formulas for the level of government support are very complex (you must spend your savings down to $3,000 etc.). For calculation purposes it is assumed the government reimburses at least 25% of total nursing home costs or $14,230 for one year.

- *With a total investment of $7,600 Lifetrack Resources and their medical care partner provided a return to client families approaching 100% four months after service is completed.*

- *Minnesota taxpayers broke even when care was delayed by six months. This return rose to 87% when nursing home care was delayed by one year.*

- *The philanthropic investor to Lifetrack Resources earned an even higher return (by at least four times) because of the leveraging impact from fee income and government grants (over 80% of revenues).*

Number of Months Nursing Home Care Avoided	2 Mos.	4 Mos.	6 Mos.	1 Year	2 Years
Nursing Home Cost	$9,500	$19,000	$28,500	$57,000	$114,000
At Least 25% of Clients on Medical Assistance	2,375	4,750	7,125	14,250	28,500
Lifetrack's Average Direct Cost Per Client Family	$5,000	—	—	—	—
Medical Costs Per Client Family	$2,600	—	—	—	—

CRITIQUE

The Lifetrack Resources analysis requires that one make assumptions about when the transition occurs from independent living to in-home assisted living, and finally to fully supportive nursing home care. Despite the tremendous expenditures by federal and state agencies for services to seniors, including nursing home care, there is little evidence that these primary funders have yet developed cost accounting systems and "age in place" services and systems that help maximize the return on investment to taxpayers. There are new initiatives aimed at insurance plans that would encourage people to save for the years when they will require nursing care support, but the numbers covered are relatively small when compared with the projected population requiring assistance. The Jay and Rose Phillips Foundation study found taxpayers savings of $2.1 million after tracking clients for only seven months following training. A longer duration tracking program initiated by state government or a private foundation may disclose even greater savings to taxpayers, as well as allow professionals to enhance their skills and learn from one another new techniques that delay the need for full-time nursing care.

Part III

WORKFORCE TRAINING PROGRAMS THAT

REDUCE SOCIAL SERVICE COSTS AND

OVER TIME RAISE TAX REVENUES

Global trade and rapid technological innovations demand that wage earners acquire new skills in a host of service, technical and managerial areas. Two-thirds of employers responding to a recent U.S. Chamber of Commerce survey indicated that shortages of skilled workers would limit their growth in the years ahead, well above the 27% response in 1993! Despite the recent slowdown in the economy most USA employers will face a labor shortage well into the 21st century. Over the next decade most states are expected to experience labor shortages, especially for skilled labor, because of underlying demographic trends. Aging is the dominant demographic trend in the USA and much of the world. Both national and international competition for the future workforce will increase dramatically in the years ahead. The working age population, ages 15-64, is growing more slowly than in the past as baby boomers exit the work force in increasing numbers. In addition, for many states like Minnesota labor-force participation rates, already among some of the highest in the nation, have likely peaked. By 2025 the number of retirement age workers is expected to exceed the number of young replacement workers entering the workforce.

On average 40% of workers make $10.00 or less per hour, the wage needed to barely sustain a family of four. Without basic skills training the gap between have and have not will increase further. The risk as stated by the Employment Policy Foundation is a USA moving from the "mass unemployment" of the 1930s to the "class unemployment" of today! The US labor market by 2030 is estimated at 165 million people or a shortfall of 35 million workers according to the Employment Policy Foundation. In addition to the need for 12-15 million additional college graduates, the USA will require 15-18 million more workers with vocational or 2-year post-secondary degrees. Underemployed individuals making very low incomes could make-up much of the labor need but they lack the education level and skills needed to meet employer requirements. In January 2007, The United States Conference of Mayors published the report "Repairing the Economic Ladder" and concluded that "baby boomer retirements will create more immediate opportunities for career-track work that pays family-supporting wages but does not require a four-year college degree."

This includes many youths who are reaching employment age without high-school degrees and also those still in high-school who need to understand and visualize the links between their current curriculum and the world of work. According to the Center for Labor Market Studies at Northeastern University (See Section Four), 46% of white students and 31% of African American students ages 16-24 who dropped out of school were unemployed in 2008. In addition, the 23% of African American students and 7% of white students ages 16-24 who had dropped out of school were incarcerated in juvenile homes, jails or prisons in 2006-2007. While the current recession makes it very difficult to connect youth to employment opportunities, leaders in the field assert that we cannot wait until the economy recovers to engage youth in the labor market. They say, "If we wait until economic conditions improve, we will have eliminated the hope of upward mobility for many in an entire generation." In addition, once the economy recovers, very large numbers of young people will be needed to fill job vacancies left by the "Baby Boom" generation.

Non-profit workforce training organizations overwhelmingly serve workers entering low-skilled jobs because government welfare policy prioritizes "work first" versus skill building. There is little funding provided for the intensive preparation required by employers for skilled, living-wage jobs. Options such as exporting jobs, downsizing or reducing growth goals will put added pressure on state budgets at a time when many residents are resistant to paying higher taxes. Significant gains in productivity will be required in future years if economic growth is to approach the historic levels of the post World War Two period.

Public policy thinking has been slow to evolve to a point where investing in future programs that prepare students or prospective workers at all ages for the world of work sits at the top of the public policy priority list. Fortunately, we now have documented evidence of how, with limited investment by public and private sources, workforce training programs can prepare and place men and women in jobs that within a short period of time more than pay back taxpayers for their investment. What has been lacking is an accounting system that accurately tracks the performance of these programs and then communicates the results to elected officials in clear and understandable language. This type of process should convince members of all political persuasions that an investment in top quality and measurable workforce training programs offers a very high return on investment. In effect it can be a money maker for the taxpayer!

It is not appropriate to compare the estimated return on investment of workforce development non-profits with one another because of wide variations in the backgrounds and skill levels of individuals served and the nature and intensity of the training programs. Assumptions have to be made about how long an individual might have remained on welfare or in the corrections system prior to employment. Also, retention rates after job placement vary especially as economic conditions change. The average cost of training is impacted by both the size of the organization and how costs are allocated to various programs. What is appropriate is to ask whether the return on investment of a particular workforce program meets an appropriate threshold of performance, given the background of the participants involved and the state of the economy that year. Variables not easily compared include differences in training cost assumptions as well as years of projected continued employment and wage level gains five and ten years into the future. Some programs clearly have more impact on an individual's future wage gains than others.

The returns derived from the reviews that follow are based on assumptions believed to be conservative and should be encouraging to elected officials and philanthropists. Where appropriate in terms of the duration of a program's impact, future returns have been adjusted to reflect the present value of current investments in the program. There are four major categories of workforce programs to be reviewed: "Welfare to Work," "Dislocated Workers," "Adult Workers," and "Youth Employment."

A study published by the Minnesota Legislative Auditor's Office in 2000 (Appendix 5) illustrates the full range of support payments and taxes paid as an individual with one dependent moves from unemployment to minimum wage, to a range of hourly wage increases up to $16.00 per hour. Using this table, the one year potential savings to taxpayers (taxes and benefits) for an individual with one dependent moving from being unemployed to earning the minimum wage of $8.00/hour would approach $9,300 excluding any savings from avoiding criminal justice system involvement. For the same individual moving from a wage of $8.00/hour to a "living wage" job at $12.00/hour, the one-year benefit to taxpayers could be as much as $8,800 excluding criminal justice system expense but including payroll taxes.

It is likely the savings would be less than stated since many individuals would likely not take advantage of all of the cash and non-cash resources available to them. Likewise, if the table in Appendix 5 could be updated to benefit levels existing in 2010, the results might indicate a different level of savings. Many existing training programs enlist both single individuals without dependents and others with more than one dependent. Since it is not always clear to what extent individuals would claim the full range of potential benefits available in the case studies which follow a 30% discount has been applied to the numbers derived from the table in Appendix 5. The purpose is to ere on the side of being conservative with the estimated savings to taxpayers. Applying the 30% discount to the "minimum wage to $12.00/hour" example above gives a net savings to taxpayers of $6,160 before adding in sales tax of $185 and criminal justice system savings of $500 for total savings of $6,845.

One of the more thorough and complex recent studies was completed in September 2009 by Raymond Robertson, professor of Economics at Macalester College and his colleague Collin Hotman (see Appendix 4). This national study included the 50 states plus the District of Columbia. Among the factors included were gains from income and sales taxes, and benefits from reduced AFDC/TANF government supports. Assumptions were also made about prospective criminal justice system costs avoided. Also their analysis varied from the Legislative Auditor's study by excluding other government supports, payroll taxes and including sales taxes and criminal justice system expense. This study estimated the benefit to taxpayers for an individual with one dependent moving from minimum wage of $7.25/hour to a "living wage job" of $12.00/hour at $7,214 for the USA as a whole and at $6,800 for the state of Minnesota (see Robinson/Hotman Workforce Study in Section Four). The Robinson study conclusion for Minnesota workers reaches about the same conclusion on savings to taxpayers as a 2007 study by the Minnesota Taxpayer's Association which concluded savings of about $6,755 but without reference to criminal justice system savings or sales tax receipts.

While each of the three studies noted above are based on slightly different inputs, I believe it is safe to conclude that taxpayer's savings would likely average about $7,000 for an individual with one dependent moving from minimum wage to $12.00/hour. For an individual moving from unemployment to minimum wage the savings would likely be close to $8,400. In the case of an individual with one dependent moving from complete unemployment to $12.00/hour the savings would be about $13,500 ($16,400 in benefits elimination less 30% plus $500 in criminal justice system costs eliminated plus $500 in sales taxes paid). The individual workforce training programs analysis that follows will apply these numbers where appropriate although at times a blended rate may be required for individuals whose wage gains do not fit neatly into the three models above.

In those cases where good data is not available on criminal justice system expense avoided, a plugged number of $500 is used which was previously published in the 1990s by the Minnesota State Planning Agency. This number is likely low since the cases where good data is available show a much higher level of savings.

One of the conclusions and recommendations going forward is that each state update a study comparable to the 2000 Minnesota Legislative Auditor study annually. This would enable timely studies to be done on the economic value of varying workforce development programs. A study should be undertaken by the State Department of Corrections in conjunction with the State Department of Employment & Economic Development to more accurately reflect the criminal justice system savings from well managed workforce training programs.

The data clearly shows that well managed programs save the taxpayer money! With the exception of HIRED (no assumed government support avoided) the following return on investment studies use assumptions that range from 1 to 5 years for the reduction in government support payments as worker incomes rise. In several cases the savings to the taxpayer more than offset the cost in the first year resulting in very attractive returns on investment. Where this is the case future return on investment calculations are based on returns after the second year of employment without applying a discounted cash flow analysis.

Since it is not clear how long an individual would have stayed on one or more government support programs in the absence of training, it is hard to calculate the duration of the estimated savings from working ones way off government support. The returns appear to be higher in the initial years immediately following training. For purposes of the estimates that follow it is assumed that future prospective wage increases are offset by a drop over time in the retention rate of those previously employed. It is likely that longer term tracking of rising incomes and consumption patterns could well increase the later year returns over what is assumed in the following studies. Intangible benefits such as the impact on family stability and healthy supporting environment for children have not been calculated.

Hired

HIRED was founded in 1968 by former criminal justice system offenders, executives from Honeywell Corporation and other private sector firms to assist individuals released from prison to relocate and find living wage jobs. It has a full range of employment services and has served over 160,000 adults and youth seeking employment in the twin cities of Minneapolis and St. Paul. In 2010 nearly 12,500 job-seekers were enrolled at HIRED. On average employment counselors place over 3,500 youth and adults in jobs each year. Performance measures include job placements, starting wages, job retention, assignments to vocational training and diploma or GED completion. The cost per placement ranges from $2,000 for a youth placement to $4,000 for an adult placement. The average wage at placement ranges from $6.73 in the Project Futures youth program to $32.90 in the GMAC dislocated worker program.

Key programs include: Welfare to Work for Low Income Parents, Dislocated Worker Training and Placement, Youth Employment and Employer Services. HIRED'S "Job Link" is a computerized job posting system currently used by over 3,500 Twin Cities employers. HIRED operates its programs through sixteen community based full service offices across the Twin City metropolitan area collaborating with public schools, correctional facilities and a wide range of other employment service providers. The staff of 180 professionals is fluent in 25 languages reflecting the growing impact of refugees and immigrants on the areas workforce. Services to refugees commenced in 1979 requiring a more diverse staff and new emphasis on training in the areas of workforce culture and literacy. Initially serving the state's growing Southeast Asian refugees, programs now include immigrants from Mexico, Somalia, the former Soviet Union, Myanmar, Laos and Turkey among others.

By investing in HIRED's "Dislocated Worker Program" taxpayers can more than recover their $4,000 investment by the end of the first year of employment saving $8,000 per successful placement. Very *high returns—$1.30 for each $1.00 invested—are earned thereafter, saving taxpayers a minimum of $1,200 annually for each successful job placement.*

The economic benefit at both the state and federal levels is actually much higher because immense costs to our economy are incurred when large numbers of people are either not in the workforce or are unemployed. These costs include: unemployment insurance benefits, welfare benefits, lost income and sales tax receipts, lower purchasing power, lost productivity, public health costs such as illness, crime, domestic violence and chemical dependency.

HIRED's YouthLEAD program returns $4.89 in benefits for every $1.00 invested, a remarkable 389% return on investment over the working career of the trainee. Every state $1.00 invested returns an estimated $14.68 over the working career of the trainee in potential savings to taxpayers, assuming a two-for-one match from other funding. Savings come from improved graduation rates, reduced special education needs and lower court and criminal justice system expenses.

MANAGEMENT

Executive Director Jane Samargia began her career with HIRED as an employment counselor in 1975. She had previously been a client experiencing the organizations adult training services. She became Executive Director in 1983 and has led the organization through multiple expansions of service with HIRED being awarded the prestigious "Recognition of Excellence Award" from the U.S. Department of Labor in 2008. Samargia, who graduated from the University of the Philippines in 1973, has a deep belief in the restorative energy of people when given a chance to improve their lot. She says, "the people we serve are from all walks of life whether a laid-off employee or a welfare parent or at risk youth, these are well-intentioned people who simply need a little assistance to find themselves on firm ground again, or perhaps for the first time in their lives." Staff is divided among the sixteen full service locations reflecting the four major program areas. Staff skills are high since many workforce programs must be custom tailored to the specific emotional and technical needs of an individual as well as the current requirements of the job market. There are nineteen members of the Board of Directors coming from key employers such as General Mills, SuperValu, Graco, Ameriprise Financial, Carlson Companies, Land O'Lakes, The Federal Reserve Bank of Minneapolis as well as leading educational and professional organizations

PROGRAM OVERVIEW....... DISLOCATED WORKERS

HIRED's dislocated worker services provides individuals experiencing a layoff with industry-specific training and education in business sectors such as advanced manufacturing, technology, financial services and health care. Nearly 2,000 dislocated workers are placed each year. In addition to new skill development the program provides assistance in career planning, analyzing transferable skills, training in current job search techniques, accessing Job Link (HIRED's proprietary job-search database) and one on one employment counseling that continues until the individual is successfully placed. More than 90% of those who complete HIRED's dislocated worker program find employment. In recent years HIRED assisted large worker layoffs from 3M, Ford Motor Company, Consolidated Precision Products (CPP), Cummins Engine, Hutchinson Technology Inc, International Paper, Musicland, North Mermorial/Park Nicollet, Seagate Technology, Best Buy, Champion Air, Northwest Airlines, Sheraton Corp., Old Home Foods, ConAgra Foods and GMAC Residential Capital..

CALCULATING THE RETURN ON INVESTMENT

The per capita cost for the dislocated worker program funded by the State of Minnesota totals $4,000. The average wage at placement is $21.85 per hour or $45,760 per year. Experience shows that the dislocated worker would have spent an additional year unemployed and started a new job earning $6,000 less in wages without HIRED's assistance. About $8,000 in federal and state taxes would therefore have been collected in the first year with additional taxes of $1,200 each year thereafter. Because of the high volume of clients and placements HIRED's per capita participant costs are relatively low. Since these are experienced workers no savings are computed from criminal justice system avoidance or government assistance. The taxpayer gains $8,000 in the first year of employment and

$1,200 for each year thereafter. Given these assumptions, training costs are more than recovered in the first year of employment ($4,000/$8,000), giving taxpayers a $2.00 return on each $1.00 invested. Ongoing taxpayer savings of $1,200 annually continue for as long as the individual is employed. HIRED is nearly 100% funded by revenues earned from government contracts, so philanthropic contributions offer an extremely high return on investment.

Assumptions:
Individual Type = Adult Dislocated Worker
Goal = Return to work at or near prior wages
Cost Per Placement = $4,000
Earnings at placement = $45,760 or $21.85/hour
Total Earnings Gain = $6,000/year plus first year gain of $45,760
Gain from MN Taxes = $2,500 year one; $400/year thereafter
Gain from USA Taxes = $5,500 year one; $800/year thereafter

Per Capita		Annually
Summary of Savings	**Year 1**	**Ongoing**
Total Earnings Gain	$45,760	$6,000
Gain from MN Taxes	2,500	400
Gain from USA Taxes	5,500	800
Total Savings	$8,000	$1,200

Cost per Placement $4,000		
Return per $1.00 Invested	$2.00	$.30
ROI	100%	30%

PROGRAM OVERVIEW & ROI ANALYSIS

YOUTH EMPLOYMENT

Very little has been written about youth employment programs in comparison to the broad range of adult programs. For that reason more than the usual space will be devoted to this program's description and ROI analysis. HIRED's youth program participants generally live in the most economically distressed neighborhoods of the Twin Cities. Their communities are overwhelmed by foreclosed homes and poorly maintained housing. Few of their neighbors are employed, many of their peers have dropped out of school, and their sidewalks and street corners are controlled by gang members and drug traffickers. While some HIRED youth have previously succumbed to lifestyles involving crime or early pregnancy, many program participants go unnoticed in their communities. They are caught in a sort of social limbo—not elevated to star status because of exceptional athletic or academic talents, and not yet deeply engaged in some of the worst elements of neighborhood life. Due to economic and social conditions, very few program participants can find jobs without extensive assistance.

"Studies show a direct benefit of early work experience for teens," writes Linda Harris of the Center for Law and Social Policy in her 2005 article "What's a Youngster to Do? The Education and Labor Market Plight of Youth in High Poverty Communities." *"Work experience in the junior or senior year of high school adds to wages in the later teen years and to increased annual earnings through age 26 especially for those not attending four-year colleges.* Youngsters in high-poverty communities are disadvantaged by their lack of early work exposure during the critical years when they should be building their labor market attachment, their workplace skills, and a portfolio of experiences that would allow them to progress."

In many ways, HIRED's youth counselors negate the breakdown of the education, community and economic infrastructure noted earlier by Linda Harris. To that end, HIRED's comprehensive youth programs effectively address the need for low-income, disadvantaged young people to be prepared for the future workforce. Through skills training, educational support, work experience and one-to-one mentoring from professional youth counselors, the youth programs prepare hundreds of program participants each year to be effective students, workers, family members and citizens. HIRED maintains that the one-to-one attention that we provide youth is crucial to their ongoing engagement in positive education, training and employment activities. Consider case notes regarding Kyle:

"Kyle is now a 19 year old African American male who enrolled with HIRED as a youth offender. Kyle came to HIRED with no high school diploma and no formal job experience. Since working with his HIRED counselor, Kyle has returned to school to receive his diploma. After high school he plans to attend community college for a degree, but he is unsure of his future career path. His counselor helped him complete the "What

Career Fits You" and "Self Directed Search" assessments, and has planned additional assessments and career exploration activities with him. The HIRED counselor also worked with Kyle on completing job applications, resumes, goal setting and work etiquette. The counselor also conducted several mock interviews and practice applications with him. Kyle has obtained a job at a sandwich shop. He likes his job and has expressed gratitude to his HIRED counselor for the assistance and the opportunity to work."

HIRED's comprehensive approach to youth employment and training programs continues to produce exceptional employment and educational outcomes for disadvantaged young people. For example, the City of Minneapolis awarded HIRED grades of "A" or "A-" in all four quarters of their youth employment and training program in 2009. HIRED also achieved notable results in the large YouthLEAD program funded by Ramsey County last year. Regarding services for youth ages 14-18, 97% of youth served attained basic, work readiness or occupational skills exceeding the goal of 85%. Eighty-seven percent of younger participants earned a high school diploma or GED, exceeding the goal of 68%. Regarding outcomes for older youth ages 19 - 21, 66% of youth received a credential within 6 months of exiting the program, exceeding the goal of 47%. Older youth achieved a $3,753 earnings change in 6 months, well above the goal of $3,100. The annual cost per participant in HIRED's Youth LEAD program is about $2,000.

CALCULATING THE RETURN ON INVESTMENT

Comprehensive youth intervention programs, such as those implemented by HIRED, can produce a significant return on investment. The report "Analyzing the Social Return on Investment in Youth Intervention Programs: A Framework for Minnesota," published in March 2007 by Paul Anton of Wilder Research and Judy Temple of the University of Minnesota notes, "An effective comprehensive program costing around $2,000 per participant returns benefits of $4.89 for every dollar of cost, based on very conservative assumptions about effects and valuations. Moreover, the program returns $14.68 for every State dollar invested, assuming a 2 to 1 match of other funding." The report details the potential return on investment for an "extensive program of mentoring and other programmatic help" for youth involved in the criminal justice system, with a cost per participant of $2,000.

Projected, specific cost savings included:

Improved high school graduation (lifetime earnings):	$7,310
Enhanced school achievement:	$1,064
Reduced initial court costs:	$ 675
Reduction cost of treatment:	$ 402
Reduced school expenses:	$ 300
Reduced juvenile crime:	$ 36
Total benefits (per student)*	$9,786
Cost of YouthLEAD program (per student)	$2,000
Benefit-cost ratio:	4.89

*Benefits based upon "A Framework for Minnesota" published in March 2007 by Paul Anton of Wilder Research and Judy Temple of the University of Minnesota

CRITIQUE

Technology has played an important role in all of HIRED's employment programs. HIRED pioneered the concept of matching prospective employee skill and experience with employer job requirements, both soft and hard skills, via the internet. With respect to youth employment the results to date speak for themselves and could well become a national role model. As is the case with other workforce programs, if some state and federal funds could be set aside for results tracking it is likely that well-managed programs would be expanded, as the savings to taxpayers would be more accurately documented. Analysis conducted by The Center for Labor Market Studies at Northeastern University (see Section Four) illustrates the economic cost to taxpayers when students drop out of high school without the skills and know how of presenting themselves for work.

Summit Academy OIC

African American males represent one of the largest groups of unemployed, both nationally and in Minnesota. Summit Academy OIC (originally, Twin Cities Opportunities Industrialization Center) is one of the leaders in moving young men of color with "at-risk" backgrounds into the workforce. The profile of Summit's enrollees is: 72% male, 73% African American, 84% unemployed, 76% twenty-one to fifty-four years of age, 19% ex-offenders and 20% having dependents. Gains in earned income and reductions in social service and criminal justice system costs are extremely high. Summit has been a leader in advocating for fairness in workforce representation for African Americans and other people of color. Companies that have provided career opportunities for Summit's trainees include: Mortenson Construction, Thor Construction, Stock Roofing, Viet Construction, Freemont Community Clinics and North Point Health & Wellness Center. Labor partnerships include The International Brotherhood of Electrical Workers (Local 292), Laborers (Local 563), Carpenter & Joiners (Local 1644) and Operating Engineers (Local 49). Other community partnerships are with Hennepin County, City of Minneapolis, Dunwoody College of Technology, MilleLacs Band of Ojibwe, American Indian OIC and HIRE Minnesota.

Summit breaks even on its training costs in the third year after an individual is placed in a job. For the five-year period following training, the estimated return is 80% ($1.80 for every $1.00 invested). For individual and governmental investors who benefit from the leveraging effect of other investors much higher returns are earned with the individual investor achieving returns exceeding 100% one year after training.

MANAGEMENT

Louis King has served as the president and CEO of Summit Academy OIC since 1993. His commitment is to create stronger communities by providing programs which emphasize self-sufficiency, responsibility, accountability and leadership development. His credo has always been that "the best social service program is a job!" He has taken the lead in insuring that major public projects comply with the law in terms their commitment to hiring people of color. At the same time he has built training programs that insure that his graduates are work-ready with both soft and hard skills. He has served on the Minneapolis School Board, The Fairview Medical Foundation Board and Network for Better Futures Board of Directors. He has participated in two White House Conferences on Children and Families, achieved certification from Harvard University on Non-Profit Management and serves as consultant to leading community based organizations and governmental entities in the Twin Cities. King is a graduate of Morehouse College and retired from the US Army with the rank of major. Summit Academy has a staff of 42 and is organized with line functions that support its training for the construction trades and health care industry as well as a range of programs that educate enrollees in the behavioral requirements for healthy independent living including adult life education. Support functions include job placement, human resources, financial aid, marketing, recruitment, finance and development. The fifteen member Board of Directors includes executives from Target Corporation, Cargill, United Healthcare, Thrivent Financial, General Mills, Q West and leading local public relations, construction, legal and manufacturing organizations.

PROGRAM OVERVIEW

Believing that "the best social service is a living-wage job," SAOIC strengthens community by preparing individuals to assume their roles as workers, parents and citizens. For over thirty years "SAOIC" has provided vocational training, basic education, counseling and job placement services to more than 20,000 people. In 2010 more than 450 adults were enrolled at SAOIC and 168 adults were placed in jobs. "Vocational Training" courses are offered in computer applications, pre-apprentice carpentry and office systems. On-site MFIP counselors work individually with students to help them accomplish their goal of economic self-sufficiency. They also assist clients to address potential barriers to training and employment such as transportation, housing and childcare. "Job Placement and Retention" specialists help students develop a resume, practice interview techniques, identify sources of job opportunities and find living wage jobs. Contact and training continues after students are placed. Summit is a leader in innovative training and job placement in the construction and health care industries.

CALCULATING THE RETURN ON INVESTMENT

In the fiscal year ending June 30, 2010, Summit Academy OIC successfully placed 168 individuals in living-wage jobs in an admittedly difficult economic environment. The net cost per successful job placement was $22,680. These workers were placed in living-wage jobs averaging nearly $13.00 per hour, resulting in an annual earnings gain of $19,000. Estimates of reductions in government support come from the Minnesota Legislative Auditor report dated January 2002 (Appendix 5). Reductions in government support reflect the fact that sixty-six of those placed in jobs were able to increase their income and move off of a public assistance payment of $12,060. Total per capita savings of $11,800 has been discounted by 30% to reflect the likelihood that applicants do not usually apply for all of the available benefits offered.

Estimates for savings in the criminal justice system are higher for Summit than for many other workforce training programs because 19% of those placed were at risk of reentry into the criminal justice system. Based on numbers from the Minnesota Department of Corrections per capita incarceration costs are estimated to be $31,000 per year. On average, incarceration costs savings were $5,840 per successful job placement. Summit has an attractive job retention rate of 80% after the first year employed; therefore, subsequent years of earnings gains as well as the benefits from lower welfare support, higher taxes and estimated savings in the criminal justice system have been discounted by this amount. Finally, a 3% discount rate has been applied to the present value analysis to reflect the real value of the current benefit of future savings for the taxpayer.

- *Summit breaks even on its costs in year three following employment delivering a return of nearly 80% to the community over five years. For the initial five year period an annual average return of 16% is earned ($40,500/$22,685/5).*

- *The philanthropic investor (26% of training costs) more than breaks even in the first year ($22,680 X 26% = $5,900) because of the leverage effect of government investment, earning a return exceeding 100% ($13,300/$5,900).*

- *Local, state and federal governments share 74% of training costs and break even in year two (74% X $22,680 = $16,800). By year five, reflecting the leverage effect of philanthropic investors, they would have earned a return of 141% or an average annual return over the five year period of 28% ($40,500/$16,800/5).*

CALCULATING THE RETURN ON INVESTMENT

Assumptions:

Goal = Living wage job

Government support years avoided = 5

Incarceration years avoided (for 32 trainees) = 1

Family size = 3

Average cost per placement ($3.81mm/168) = $22,680

Total trainees placed per year = 168

Pre training wage 127 individuals $2.00/hour (part time workers)

Pre training wage 41 individuals $8.00/hour (full time workers)

Post training wage 127 individuals = $12.00/hour (full time)

Post training wage 41 individuals = $ 16.00/hour (full time)

Average reduction in government support (127) = $18,000

Average reduction in government support 41) = $13,000

Total average reduction in government support = 16,800

Reduction in government support X 70% = $11,800

Gain from State & Federal Taxes = $1,100

Gain from State Sales Tax = $400

Elimination of Justice System Costs (32 x $30,641/168) = $5,840

Per Capita Taxpayer Savings	1 Yr	2 Yrs	3 Yrs	5 Yrs
Total Earnings Gain	$19,000	$38,000	$57,000	$95,000
Reduction in Government Support	5,960*	17,760	28,060	51,360
Gain from USA & State Income Tax	1,100	2,200	3,300	5,500
Gain from Sales Tax	400	800	1,200	2,000
Justice System Savings	5,840	1,500	300	---
Total Savings	$13,300	$22,260	$32,860	$58,860
Adjust for 80% Retention		$17,800	$24,100	$47,100
Present Value @3%		$16,800	$22,100	$40,500

PV / Per Placement Cost ($22,685)		1.79
Average Annual ROI		16%

* $11,800 net of $5,840 one year criminal justice system expense.

CRITIQUE

Summit offsets a heavy investment in training costs with higher than average placement wages for many of the "hardest to employ" individuals. Summit's advocacy for public sector projects to fulfill minority hiring commitments is somewhat unique among workforce development programs. Returns for Summit are likely understated since while placing many of the hardest to employ in $12.00/hour jobs, many with criminal backgrounds, they also lift existing $8.00/hour employees totally off of income support to jobs paying up to $18.00/hour. A true wild card is the assumption on how many years an individual may have remained in the criminal justice system had they not gained employment through Summit's program. Wages are conservatively projected as being flat going forward. There is really no way to compute all of these prospective savings more accurately without a longitudinal study, which while costly initially, could over time be part of the state's ongoing annual workforce performance measurement system.

Goodwill Easter Seals

Goodwill Easter Seals Minnesota scores as a very high return-on-investment workforce development center in part because of the high percentage of its in revenues derived from earned income. Goodwill Easter Seals has been a significant contributor to Minnesota's workforce for more than 90 years. Their programs help people prepare for work, train for employment, obtain jobs, maintain employment, advance careers and connect to community resources. Clientele include individuals with mental and chemical health issues, ex-offenders, refugees and new Americans, low income and fragile families, at-risk youth and dislocated workers.

By investing in Goodwill Easter Seals' Skills Training program, philanthropic investors and government can more than recover their investment by the end of the first year and achieve very high returns thereafter saving the taxpayer about $8,300 for each successful job placement that eliminated dependence on government support. Each dollar invested in GWES returns $1.57 after the first year of employment or a 57% ROI after returning the initial investment. Thereafter, returns of at least 20% annually are generated as long as the individual is working.

Goodwill's retail operations generated over $38 million in sales for the Minnesota economy in 2010 serving 2.6 million store customers. That year 1,036 program participants went to work and 164 gained career advancement. In recent years $11.34/hour average starting wage has been achieved for skills training graduates. The program generates more than $17 million in taxable income earned by participants that gained employment. Program funding is a mixture of government and private grants, fees for service and revenues generated from Goodwill retail stores. On average $4.00 in private funds are leveraged from each $1.00 received from the State of Minnesota.

MANAGEMENT

Michael Wirth Davis has served as president and CEO of Goodwill Easter Seals since 1990. He previously was director of education and vocational services at the famed Courage Center in Minnesota, and before that, director of adult services at the Ray Graham Association in Elmhurst, Illinois. He has written numerous publications dealing with human developmental issues as well as best practices in the management of not-for-profit human service organizations. He has spoken extensively on the subject of rehabilitation and been recognized and honored by numerous organizations for his leadership in the field of workforce readiness for disadvantaged individuals. Reporting to Davis are the directors of mission services, finance, retail services, development & marketing and human resources. The 21 members on the board of directors includes representatives from Wells Fargo, Supervalu, Macy's, 3M, Campbell Mithun Esty, The Minneapolis Community Foundation, University of Minnesota, University of Wisconsin and several other for-profit organizations.

PROGRAM OVERVIEW

From 18 locations 925 employees provide state-wide services to Minnesotans with disabilities and disadvantages. Paid-work experience is provided in the retail stores and at the corporate headquarters. More than 1,000 people with multiple barriers to work were placed in jobs in 2010. In addition to the basic career workforce model English Language Learning, mathematics, parenting, life skills, and housing retention classes are provided. The industry cluster skills training program, developed in partnership with Minnesota businesses, provides curriculum-based and hands on training serving the automotive, construction, retail, banking and financial services industries. Long term follow-up and support services help both participants and employers. The community resource staff provides housing resources, retail vouchers for clothing, medical equipment loans and one-on-one assistance. In 2010, 755 ex-offenders were assisted in their transition from prison to employment.

CALCULATING THE RETURN ON INVESTMENT

Using the table prepared by the Minnesota State Auditor (Appendix 5) one can see that pre training earnings of $4.15 per hour are just above the "not working" benefit column. Placement earnings of $11.34 are just under the $12.00 per hour level. Therefore, we will assume that total government support declined by about $13,000. The primary drivers of these changes were Section 8 Housing, MFIP/AFDC and MFIP Food Assistance. It is assumed that prospective welfare recipients would not have qualified for all of the government assistance programs and therefore total potential support of $13,000 has been discounted by 30%. The auditor's table shows a gain of about $650 from state and federal income taxes. Assuming 30% of the income gain of $14,400 is spent and qualifies for the sales tax at 6.5%, we can add an additional $162 to the gain in taxes. Studies indicate on average 5% of those seeking workforce training generally have long-lasting involvement with the criminal justice system. When applying this against average justice system costs an additional gain of $500 can be added to the benefit column. Therefore, $8,300 of annual benefit is obtained in the first year after job placement plus an additional $1,310 each year thereafter.

Given these assumptions, costs are more than recovered in the first year after training ($8,300/$5,300) and continue for as long as we assume the person would have continued on welfare in the absence of training. Ongoing taxpayer savings of $1,048 annually continue for as long as the individual is employed. With the State of Minnesota supporting 29% of training costs, and for the philanthropic investor providing 25% of training costs, the leverage effect would increase their returns by as much as threefold over the stated results. Income from retail operations significantly enhances the return on investment, thereby allowing other investors to benefit from the leveraging affect.

Assumptions:
Cost per placement = $5,300
Government Support Years Avoided = 1
Pre training wage = $4.15/hour
Post training placement wage = $11.34/hour
Income gained from training = $14,400/year
Reduction in federal and state support costs X 70% = $9,100
Gain from USA and state income tax = $650.
Gain from state sales tax = $162 .
Gain from avoiding criminal justice system = $500

Estimated Savings Per Capita	Year 1	Annually Ongoing
Total Earnings Gain	$14,400	$14,400
Reduction in USA & State benefits less 30%	9,100	
Gain from USA & Minnesota income taxes	650	650
Gain from Sales Tax	160	160
Justice System Savings	500	500
Total Gain	$10,410	$1,310
Adjust for 80% Retention	$8,300	$1,050
Estimated Cost Per Placement		$5,300
Year 1 Return on Investment	1.57	.20
ROI	57%	20%

CRITIQUE

The fact that Goodwill Easter Seals has been in business for many years and has creatively moved to reinvent itself when necessary speaks well for the vision of its board and the expertise of management. The assumption that trainees may only have stayed on welfare one year in the absence of training could prove to be conservative. GWES has been innovative in establishing its own revenue generating retail store network. This earned revenue substantially helps reduce the cost to the public of work-force training programs. Also for large multi program organizations the manner in which costs are allocated between programs can dramatically impact the ultimate return on investment from a particular activity. Another advantage of GWES retail business is that it allows trainees to have supervised work experience before approaching private market firms. The success of its programs also reflects the benefit of having diversity on the board of directors with significant representation from large and medium-sized businesses.

Resource

RESOURCE is one of Minnesota's leading providers of comprehensive services that empower people to achieve greater personal, social and economic success. Since its founding in 1960, RESOURCE has provided life-changing services to more than 175,000 individuals. RESOURCE is a multicultural, non-profit organization that operates over 50 specialized programs in the areas of employment and training, chemical health, mental health and a range of other disabilities. Annually nearly 950 "at risk" youth struggling to survive are served. RESOURCE provides services to over 20,000 individuals each year in the Twin Cities metropolitan area, St. Cloud and Duluth, Minnesota. RESOURCE's "welfare-to-work" programs serve annually more than 8,100 parents. In 2010 nearly 29,000 children benefited indirectly from their parents' success in working towards self-sufficiency. This analysis will focus on Hennepin County (Minnesota's largest urban county) residents who qualify for MFIP (Minnesota Family Investment Plan).

By investing in RESOURCE Hennepin County MFIP programs, philanthropic investors and government can more than recover their cost by the end of the first year, actually doubling their investment, and achieve very high returns thereafter, saving taxpayers more than $10,000 annually for each successful job placement that eliminated dependence on government support. After returning the initial investment RESOURCE'S first year ROI is 114% ($2.14 returned for each $1.00 invested) with annual returns of 12% annually for as long as the individual continues to work.

MANAGEMENT

Deborah Atterberry has served as president of RESOURCE since November 2004. She previously managed and directed (since 1978) Employment Action Center (EAC), RESOURCE's largest division. Within

EAC, Atterberry managed five divisions: Youth and Young Parent Programs, Welfare to Work Programs, Adult Workforce Programs, Women's Programs, and Dislocated Worker Programs. Atterberry initiated several national and local demonstration projects including: New Chance (a comprehensive case management program for teen mothers), SKILLS 2000 (a workplace literacy program for adults), and Young Dads (a skill-development program for young fathers). More recent innovative programs include: Career Launch (employment services for immigrants), Jobs for Veterans (employment services for returning and disabled veterans), Young Adult Housing & Employment Services (housing and employment for adults aged 18-25 with a serious mental illness) and Mothers Achieving Recovery for Family Unity Housing & Treatment Program (one of the first treatment programs in the Twin Cities to allow mothers to go through treatment without having to be separated from their children). Atterberry has earned degrees from the University of Wisconsin - Madison, and the University of St. Thomas. She was named a Woman of Achievement by the TwinWest Chamber of Commerce and has received the JOBS Now Coalition Community Service Award. RESOURCE operates with a board of 15 including executives from US Bank, General Mills, Blue Cross, United Health Group, Cargill and members from the legal, investment, construction and education professions.

PROGRAM OVERVIEW

The staff of 270 represents a wide range of cultural groups and speaks over 25 languages. It operates out of 34 sites in the Twin Cities metro area plus sites in Duluth and St. Cloud. In a typical year, the agency assists more than 3,500 laid-off workers and other unemployed or underemployed adults seeking employment and over 8,000 parents on welfare seeking self-sufficiency. Nearly 1,500 individuals grappling with substance-abuse problems are assisted, most with a history of relapse and many with prison records. In the area of mental illness, over 2,000 adults are served who are striving to live and participate actively in the community. More than 26,000 children of those served also benefit indirectly from their parents' success. Specific services include: One-on-one case management and counseling; job planning, soft skills and job search workshops; one-on- one job interview preparation; target marketing and advocacy with employers; on-site interviews at RESOURCE by prospective employers; accessing supportive funds for specialized training, uniforms, car repairs, child care and bus cards as well as career advancement and financial planning workshops.

CALCULATING THE RETURN ON INVESTMENT

This contract from Hennepin County in the amount of $1,912,650 served 1,354 MFIP recipients. After training 1,027 were able to find either part-time or full-time work. Of these, 350 were at a wage per hour level to make the family ineligible for MFIP altogether. About 650 began to work part-time or full-time still on some MFIP support. In making the per successful job placement cost estimate, the most conservative approach has been used, namely dividing $ 1,912,650 by the 350 individuals who for sure worked their way off of MFIP. In addition the assumption has been made that 513 individuals worked full time (2,000 hours/year) at $10.50 per hour and 514 individuals worked part time (1,000 hours/year) at $9.50 per hour. By averaging these two groups the total per person income gained from training amounted to $15,250 or about $7.63 per hour. Applying this wage to the Legislative Auditor's table (Appendix 5) results in government support payment savings of $13,700 or $9,590 after applying a 30% discount. The key drivers of the savings are reductions in MFIP, food stamps and housing. The standard approach (30% of income gain x 6.25%) was used to estimate sales tax receipts and criminal justice system savings ($500).

Given these assumptions, costs are more than recovered in the first year after training ($10,390/$5,500) and continue for as long as we assume the person would have continued on welfare in the absence of training. Ongoing taxpayer savings of $640 annually continue for as long as the individual is employed. Because of the leveraging effect the returns to both government and philanthropic investors are actually higher than what could be calculated from the above numbers since service fees represent 17% of income to RESOURCE and government about 75%.

Assumptions:

Goal = Eliminate need for MFIP
Government support years Avoided = 1
Family Size = Single parent with one child
Number trained and placed = 513 Full Time & 514 Part Time

Cost per placement = $5,500

Income gained from training (100% unemployed or were working part time)

     50% at $10.50/hour for 2,000 hours = $21,000/year

     50% at $9.50/hour for 1,000 hours = $9,500/year

Average income gained from training = $15,250 or $7.63/hour

Reduction in state and federal support costs = $13,700

Gain from state and federal taxes = 0

Gain from state sales tax = $300

Gain from criminal justice avoidance = $500

Per Capita Summary of Savings	Year 1		Ongoing Annually
Total Earnings Gain	$15,250		$15,250
Reduction in Government Support (less 30%)	9,590		0
Gain from Taxes	0		0
Gain from Sales Tax	300		300
Justice System Savings	500		500
Total Gain	$10,390		$800
Adjust for 80% Retention			$640
Estimated Cost Per Placement		$5,500	
Return per $1.00 invested	2.14		.12
ROI	114%		12%

CRITIQUE

The returns above reflect calculations for only one of RESOURCE's many programs under contract with various government entities. While wage levels are known for those now working, it is not clear exactly how many jobs were placed at full-time versus part-time hours worked, and therefore estimates believed to be conservative have been made. The estimate on costs reflects only the total expended on the Hennepin County MFIP contract and does not include any allocation of overhead from general management functions. Given the number of programs managed, the number is likely not large enough to substantially change conclusions about potential return on investment. Clearly the manner in which costs are allocated between programs can dramatically impact return on investment calculations. It is likely that RESOURCE's success in preparing people for work benefits greatly from its extensive in-house expertise in dealing with the full range of medical, emotional, physical and economic challenges facing its clients.

Project for Pride in Living

Project for Pride in Living was founded in 1971 by community activist Joe Selvaggio. For 40 years, PPL has helped low-income people achieve self-sufficiency. Recognized nationally by the Department of Labor and others, PPL offers an integrated range of services: employment and training, affordable housing, human support services and formal education. PPL reaches nearly 14,000 people each year by offering comprehensive programs in rental and ownership housing, employment and training, supportive services and youth development. 6,750 adults received job support in 2010. Individuals were served through six programs: "Train to Work", "PPL Industries", "PPL SHOP", "Center for Working Families", "Connections to Work" and "Skills 4 Work." PPL has expanded through both internal growth and merger. Its core mission of "helping people help themselves" has remained constant since its founding. In 1998 it was selected by the Fannie Mae Foundation as one of ten outstanding Community Development Corporations (CDCs) nationwide.

By investing in PPL's "Train to Work" programs, philanthropic investors and government can more than recover their cost by the end of the first year, returning the investors $1.33 for every $1 invested. With the initial investment more than recovered after one year of work, the ongoing savings provide an annual return on investment of 17%. The quality of training is such that the future opportunity for income gains by the trainees is high.

MANAGEMENT

Steve Cramer is Executive Director of Project for Pride in Living (PPL) having started with the organization in 1994 as director of housing and development. He was elected to the Minneapolis City Council and served as a council member from 1984 through 1993 after receiving his M.A. in Public Affairs from the Humphrey Institute of Public Affairs at the University of Minnesota and his B.S. in urban planning from the University of Tulsa. He has wide exposure in urban development having served on the boards of numerous non-profit and governmental organizations. The board of PPL is large, numbering 37, reflecting the breadth of its operations and a recent merger with representation from all key segments of the community. Revenues of the organization exceed $17 million, divided almost equally between earned income and grants and contributions. Steve Cramer has an experienced senior staff operating out of the central office and other urban based locations. Programs are run by staff assisted by volunteers from 19 leading corporate, professional and educational institutions. Cramer says, "I feel privileged to having a front row seat to see very positive events happen in the lives of individuals and families and/or the collective life of a community, and knowing I played some small role in these results."

Program Overview

Train to Work prepares inner-city residents for entry-level positions in a wide range of businesses. Classroom training includes computer skills, technical skills for clerical/administrative work and positions such as teller, proof clerk, dietary aid, linen distribution aid as well as career advancement training for incumbent health care workers who want to advance in their field. PPL operates two self-sustaining skill-building entrepreneurial businesses that offer on-the-job training: PPL Industries and PPL Shop. PPL Industries specializes in light assembly work and contracts with metro businesses to do labor intensive handwork. It teaches basic employment skills. PPL Shop sells used functional home and office furniture and building materials donated by business and individuals and has a customer base of 8,000. The Health Careers Partnership connects individuals to educational institutions such as Minneapolis Community and Technical College to study health careers and take an assessment test. The Computer Access Lab assists job seekers in writing resumes, filling out job applications, accessing community resources for family support needs and applying to colleges and technical schools including the seeking of financial aid.

Calculating The Return On Investment

PPL is placing *Train to Work* graduates in jobs at an average hourly wage of about $13.58 per hour or $27,160 per year. It is estimated that the gain in annual earnings from *Train to Work* is about $14,860 over and above what might have been earned before training reflecting the fact that only four of the 70 placed in jobs reported any income earned prior to training. The estimated gain in income taxes paid by the worker is $800 and sales taxes paid is $290. For the sales taxes paid we have assumed that 30% of the income gain is spent on sales tax related items at a 6½% rate. It is estimated that a certain percentage of those who don't find work wind up in the criminal justice system. To be conservative we use the number 1% and apply that against a low end estimate of $50,000/year corrections costs. The result is an estimated corrections savings of $500. About 47% of PPL's "Train to Work" graduates have dependents; therefore, estimated reductions in government assistance have been reduced by 30% to reflect lower savings from those without dependents resulting in net savings from assistance of $8,610.

Given these assumptions, costs are more than recovered in the first year after training ($10,200/$7,694).The taxpayer gains $1.33 in the first year of employment for each $1.00 invested and the same for each year the individual would have remained on government assistance. Ongoing taxpayer savings of $1,272 annually continue for as long as the individual is employed. Since about 60% of PPL's *Train to Work* budget is dependent on philanthropic contributions, the return to philanthropic contributors is higher than what is stated above. The balance of funding comes from government grants and fees for service performed. The return to the state of Minnesota is very high and will greatly exceed that of the philanthropic investor since there is less than $100,000 of direct aid from government in *Train to Work!*

Assumptions:
Goal = Move towards living wage job
Government Support Years Avoided = 1
Cost per Placement = $ 7,694
Average Pre training wage   = $6.15/hour
Average Post training wage = $13.58/hour
Income gained from training = $14,860
Reduction in Government Support = $12,300
Gain from Income Tax = $800
Gain from Sales Tax = $290
Justice System Savings = $500

Per Capita Summary of Savings	Year 1	Ongoing Annually
Total Earnings Gain	$14,860	$14,860
Reduction in Government Support Less 30%	8,610	
Gain from Income Taxes	800	800
Gain from Sales Tax	290	290
Justice System Savings	500	500
Total Savings	$10,200	$1,590
Adjusted for 80% Retention		$1,272
Estimated Cost per Placement	$7,694	
Return per $1.00 invested	1.33	.17
ROI	33%	17%

CRITIQUE

Project for Pride in Living has successfully transitioned from the entrepreneurial phase of its original focus on affordable housing to its current status as a large well-established organization with expertise in building affordable housing, job skill training, retailing, light assembly manufacturing and education. The breadth of its operations offers prospective workforce entrants a range of skill building opportunities. The economics of scale also helps to keep training costs relatively low. A key lesson learned from its successful "Train to Work" program is the enormous benefits to be gained from partnering with a leading hospital system and community college in relatively close proximity to one another. The organization is particularly well skilled at involving leaders in nearly all sectors of the community in its work.

Twin Cities Rise!

Founded in 1994 by former General Mills executive, Steve Rothschild, Twin Cities Rise! (TCR!) offers a high return on investment to its sponsors. TCR! fills a gap in the continuum for training and educating individuals. It provides intensive skills training for the very hard-to-employ poor not served by many non-profit placement programs or higher educational institutions. Its unique market-based training serves the employer as its customer, insuring that its graduates fill needed jobs at living wages. Graduates can earn living wage salaries of $25,000 or higher. TCR!'s impressive retention rate of 82% through 12 months on the job and 71% after 24 months beats the experience of its employer customers, insuring that employers save expense from reduced turnover. Self-development programs focus on accountability and personal empowerment. The ability to train a client to believe in oneself and visualize a future is critical to success. TCR!'s "personal empowerment program" has been perfected and spun out as a separate profit center, marketed and available to others in the work force training field.

This study shows that TCRise's total economic benefit to the community averages 18% annually for the five years following an individual's training and job placement. Reflecting the leverage provided by philanthropic contributors and earned income, an independent study by professors at Macalester College in September of 2009 concluded that the State of Minnesota achieved returns exceeding 400% ($5.00 for every $1.00 invested) since its initial TCR! investment in 1997.

MANAGEMENT

President and CEO, Arthur Berman spent the early part of his working career in the private sector as an executive with American Express and Ameriprise Financial Services after first serving with the Environmental Protection Agency and the consulting firm, Booze Allen and Hamilton. A graduate of Bowdin College and the Wharton School of Finance at the

University of Pennsylvania, Berman had developed an interest in the analytics surrounding public policy decisions and became an early advocate for applying return-on- investment concepts to both governmental and corporate decision making. Reporting to Berman are the chief operating officer and directors for development, empowerment institute and finance. Reporting to COO Shelley Jacobson are program directors for coaching, employer services, volunteer services, recruiting, technology and education services. The board of directors includes executives from Opus, Wells Fargo, Faegre & Benson, Honeywell International, Mortenson Construction, Super Valu, Travelers Insurance, Medtronic, General Mills, Littler & Mendelson, Metropolitan State University, Greater Twin Cities United Way, Hennepin County Court System, Minneapolis City Council and the Wilder Foundation.

PROGRAM OVERVIEW

Twin Cities Rise! training programs focus on class work and coaching in personal responsibility, conflict resolution, negotiation and problem solving. Work skills include basic computer training, communication skills, critical thinking, customer service and dealing with change and business growth. A "coach" is assigned to each participant throughout training, during the time the applicant seeks a full-time job and during the entire first year of employment. Participants progress through the program in four or more ten- week phases committing to 12-15 hours of training per week. In 2010, TCR! served more than 2,000 participants in all of its programs. TCR! ranks as one of the leading job training providers for living-wage positions, jobs paying $25,000 or more, in the Twin Cities. Each participant signs a contract committing to one year employment with a TCR! customer of their choosing at full wages and benefits. TCR! believes that its unique financial and skills training model insures accountability and positive outcomes.

CALCULATING THE RETURN ON INVESTMENT

Funded primarily by private contributions TCR! receives only about 19% of its revenue from state government. The government contract gives TCR! $9,000 per trainee upon successful job placement and an additional $9,000 if the trainee is still employed one year later. CEO, Art Berman points out that with this kind of "pay for performance" arrangement the state cannot lose as it pays TCR! only for success, and success guarantees a high return for the state. He estimates that the benefits of increased tax revenue from new employees and the decrease in public assistance and incarceration expenses more than offset the state's portion of the training costs offering the state more than a 400% return on its investment, with a payback period of about two years. TCR! pioneered the concept of "pay for performance," advocating this approach at both the federal and state levels of government. In their opinion it creates a discipline that inspires both quality and efficiency in their work.

To compute the average cost per successful job placement, we will refer to a detailed analysis done in 2008 which showed that 416 of 640 individuals in the program were employed either full-time or part-time. Of these, 60 achieved the highest rating getting placed in jobs earning $25,000 or more per year plus benefits; 70 found full-time or part-time jobs at lower hourly rates, and the balance either remained in training or left the program. The average earnings of those entering the program was about $3,000, reflecting some with part-time work experience as well as others with criminal backgrounds. Therefore, the gain in income as a result of training ranged from $7,500 to $21,000. The average cost per successful placement is estimated to be $19,650 (total grants and contributions allocated for training divided by the number of successful placements).

Using the table prepared by the Minnesota state auditor in 2002 (Appendix 5) we can see that average pre-training earnings of $3,000, is close to the "not working" category. We will assume that government support dropped by $12,000 for the 60 high earning graduates and by $8,000 for the lower earning group of 70, or an overall average savings of about $9,800. Total savings of $9,800 has been discounted by 30% to reflect the likelihood that applicants do not usually apply for all of the available benefits offered. The auditor's table shows a gain of about $400 per graduate from income taxes. Assuming 30% of income/spending qualifies for the sales tax at 6.5%, we can add an additional $340 to the gain in taxes. TCR! calculates that its program reduces the recidivism rate for ex-offender participants well below the national average. The assumption is that 5% of TCR! trainees are at risk of becoming incarcerated. Applying this assumption to an estimated one year of potential prison time, at a daily cost of $103, results in average criminal justice savings of $1,450 for each trainee. This estimate is likely low as reduced recidivism rates could well apply to the additional 500 or more individuals who participated in the program.

The analysis shows TCR! breaking even on its total investment in the third year following job placement and delivering a 90% return to the community over five years ($1.90 for each $1.00 invested) or an average annual return of 18%. Since philanthropic investors' contributions comprise more than one half of training costs their returns would be higher approaching 25% per year over a five year period.

The return calculated by the "Robertson/Hotmann Study" in Appendix 4 shows a return exceeding 400% for the state's investment, in part because it benefits from the leveraging effect of the state's investment only representing 19% of the total. The time frame for their calculation is different as they use a data base that differs from the calculations derived in the state auditor's study of 2002.

Assumptions:
Goal = living wage job
Government support years avoided = 5
Incarceration years avoided (for 5% of trainees) = 1
Total trainees placed per year = 130
Average Cost per placement ($2.55MM/130) = $19,650
Pre training wage 60 individuals = $2.25 per hour (part time workers)
Pre training wage 70 individuals = $1.10 per hour (part time workers)
Post training placement wage 60 individuals = $12.65 per hour (full time)
Post training wage 70 individuals = $5.00 per hour (part time workers)
Average Income gained from training = $13,750/year
Reduction in government support X 70% = $9,800
Gain from USA and state income tax = $400.
Gain from state sales tax = $340 or 2% of income gain
Gain from avoiding criminal justice system (5%x$103x365/130) = $1,450

Per Capita Taxpayer Savings	1 Yr	2Yrs	3Yrs	5Yrs
Reduction in Gov't Assistance	$9,800	$19,600	$29,400	$49,000
Gain from USA & State Income Tax	400	800	1,200	2,000
Gain from Sales Tax	340	680	1,020	1,700
Justice System Savings	1,450	300	----	----
Total Savings	$11,990	$21,380	$31,620	$52,700
Adjust for 80% Retention		$17,531	$25,300	$42,600
Present Value @3%		$16,525	$23,730	$37,276
PV/Per Placement Cost ($19,650)			1.21	1.90
Average Annual ROI				18%

CRITIQUE

Twin Cities Rise! has pioneered "pay for performance" contracting, which is changing the way government-financed workforce training program contracts are awarded and evaluated. The fact that the TCR! data includes recidivism statistics is also a major contribution to return on investment calculations for workforce programs. If this data were more broadly used the returns on many work force programs would likely be higher. It is assumed that because of almost no prior work experience that TCR! trainees would have remained on government assistance for five years prior to training. The long-term returns are likely higher than those shown above since TCR!'s specialized training not only secures an attractive starting wage job, but also equips trainees with a very high probability for significant future wage advancement.

Section Two

National Programs with High Returns on Investment

Many excellent programs that lend themselves to ROI analysis are national in scope, or on the verge of going national. Some have emerged from successful local programs that have been brought to scale, while others grew from pilot programs launched by public policy institutes. This section examines five such efforts. Several have track records long enough to provide highly creditable evidence of success. Each of the case studies that follow presents the prospect of significant improvement in taxpayer-funded services, while at the same time applying scarce financial resources in a more efficient manner.

The Benefits of High Quality Early Childhood Education

The Minnesota Department of Education has found that only 50% of Minnesota children are fully prepared to enter kindergarten. This finding has national implications, since by most measures Minnesota ranks at or near the top in educational performance. When children are not fully prepared to enter kindergarten, their progress in grade school and high school is impeded. Numerous studies (Chicago, Michigan, North Carolina) now prove that the lack of affordable and accessible quality early childhood programs creates an unnecessary large financial burden for future taxpayers. A 2005 Bush Foundation study concluded that approximately 111,000 Minnesota children from birth to five years live in poverty. Only about 45% of these are being served with early childhood programs. To reach more children, the critical needs are greater physical access to quality child care, a user friendly quality rating system of child care providers and financial support to needy families that ensures that quality care is affordable. With the exception of Head Start, Minnesota and most other states lack a broad based, systematic, sustainably funded infrastructure for assuring high quality pre-kindergarten preparation or even an agreed-upon definition of quality beyond basic licensure and accreditation regulations.

Legislative cuts since 2003 to early childhood programs have exacerbated existing problems in the availability and affordability of care, especially for low-income families. For children in licensed child care, government licensing standards are at a minimum-level quality assurance. Even when care is licensed, it is not a guarantee of high-quality care. In a 2003 study, licensed child care centers averaged between above "minimal" and below "good." As of 2001 only 43 percent of U.S. 3-year-olds and 66% of 4-year-olds were enrolled in some form of preschool programs according to a RAND Corporation study. The federal government funds Head Start, which serves about 900,000 3 to 4-year-olds each year. Thirty-eight states provide funding for an additional 700,000 children, predominantly 4-year-olds considered to be disadvantaged. Only Georgia and Oklahoma have programs available to all 4-year-olds. Enrollment rates are lower in communities of color and still lower for families with incomes below the poverty line. Only 38 percent of 3 to 5-year-olds whose mothers had less than a high school education were enrolled in early education programs, compared with 70 percent of those whose mothers had at least a college degree. State preschool programs vary considerably in quality and dollars invested. Twelve of the thirty-eight states with programs met fewer than five of the ten quality standards set by the National Institute on Early Education Research (NIEER). Only half of the state programs (20 out of 38) require the lead classroom teacher to have a bachelor's degree which is required in every state kindergarten program.

The benefits of high quality early childhood education are many. Children benefit by having higher test scores at ages five, six, nine and fourteen and higher graduation rates than non-participating students. Taxpayers benefit directly from higher rates of home ownership, income and sales taxes paid and reduced social service and criminal justice system expense, as documented in the Perry study of participant's economic status by age 27. Employers benefit. The Business Roundtable states that higher quality employees are recruited and retained when assistance is provided allowing better access to high quality early childhood programs. Local, state and the federal government benefits when the cycle of poverty is broken for low income families and scarce resources can be devoted to programs that strengthen regional economies in this very competitive international economy. Leaders in the field agree that early childhood education must begin in the home at birth. They also agree that the largest economic payoff comes from adequately preparing youth from our poorest families with intensive targeted high quality educational services. The key is quality service, which comes with a cost; however, the payoff can be huge and render dividends well into a child's adult life.

What follows are two separate longitudinal studies performed over different time periods followed by a state study that applied its specific demographics to one of the studies to reach its own conclusion about the cost/benefit ratio of high quality early childhood education.

HIGH/SCOPE PERRY PRESCHOOL STUDY

One of the most comprehensive longitudinal studies of the benefits of early childhood education was initiated in Yipsilanti, Michigan in 1962. It is known to educators as the "High/Scope Perry Pre-School Study."

From 1962 to 1965, 123 African American preschool-age (ages 3-4) children born in poverty and at high risk of failing in school were identified. Their educational, social and economic performance was tracked to age 27. Evenly matched as to socioeconomic status and mean intellectual performance, 58 of these children were placed in a preschool program, with the remaining 65 not enrolled in a preschool program. From October to June, program teachers conducted daily 2.5-hour classes for children on weekday mornings and made 1.5-hour home visits to each mother and child on weekday afternoons. Using experiences taken from child development theory, adults encouraged children to participate in actions where they learned to make choices, solve problems and perform in a manner that stimulates their intellectual, social and physical development. At age 27 the data collector interviewed 95% of the original study participants and these results are posted in the "Return on Investment" section which follows.The study phases included data collection at ages 19, 27 and 39-41.

More recent studies confirm similar positive results. Launched in 2003, the Early Literacy AmeriCorps Program was designed to develop the literacy skills of Head Start children. Dramatic gains have been documented in such skills as picture naming, rhyming and alliteration, each essential in preparing children to read. The Yipsilanti study is by far the most comprehensive to date. Arthur Rolnick and Rob Grunewald, economists with the Ninth Federal Reserve District in Minneapolis, Minnesota, researched the study and in January 2003 published the following conclusion:

"Based on present value estimates, about 80% of the benefits (from the Perry School program) went to the general public yielding over a 12% internal rate of return for society in general."

The methodology used by Rolnick and Grunewald to calculate the rate of return on the initial dollars invested in the program estimated the time periods in which costs and benefits in constant dollars were paid or received by program participants and society. The High/Scope

Educational Research Foundation reviewed the results of the study in April, 2003, converting the financial impact of the program into 2001 dollars. The discounted average cost of the program was calculated to be $14,716 per participant. Based on the typical in-court and out-of-court settlements, $68,584 was saved by the potential victims of crimes that were avoided and never committed; $15,240 was estimated to be saved in reduced justice system costs (arrests, investigation, court and incarceration expense); $7,488 was saved in schooling, due to reduced need for special educational services, even after allowing for increased college costs for preschool-program participants; $3,475 was saved through reduced welfare costs and $10,537 was the gain from increased taxes paid by preschool-program participants because of their higher earnings.

In 2001 dollars the total financial benefits of the Perry Pre School Program amounted to $105,324 per participant by age 27. Divided by the cost of $14,716 per participant the percentage return on investment (after subtracting the original cost) exceeded 600%. Because the costs of the program are incurred at the start and the benefits to the individual and society come much later, the computed internal rate of return is lower than what would simply be derived from dividing the 600% total return by the twenty-four-year interval from age 3 to age 27. Rolnick and Grunewald estimated the time periods in which costs and benefits occurred and that is how they concluded that a 12% internal rate of return was earned for society in general.

SURVEY RESULTS AT AGE 27
SHOWING THE IMPACT OF PRE- KINDERGARTEN
TRAINING (IN 2001 DOLLARS)

	Non-Program Group	Program Group	Program Group Economic Benefit
Economic			$11,000 (Tax Revenue) $3,000 (No Welfare)
Earning $24,000 by age 27	7%	29%	
Own their home	13%	36%	$59.0
Never on welfare as an adult	20%	41%	$142.0
Educational			$7,000 (Special education)
Ever treated for mental impairment	34%	15%	
Age 14 achieve in 10th percentile	15%	66%	
Graduated high school on time	45%	66%	
Criminal Justice			$15,000
(Crime victims) mean number of arrests	4.6	2.3	$69,000

Total savings per student of $105,324 divided by the discounted cost per student of $14,716 results in a total return on investment of 616% by age 27 for each program group student ($7.16 Saved for each $1.00 Invested).

THE CHICAGO CHILD-PARENT CENTER PROGRAM

The work of the center and the benefits of quality early education programs were published recently in the Journal of the American Medical Association's Archives of Pediatrics & Adolescent Medicine. This research was led by University of Minnesota professors Arthur Reynolds and Judy Temple. The Chicago Longitudinal Study has been following a sample of 1,539 children born in 1980 from low socioeconomic families. The 989 children who completed the Chicago CPC pre-K program and kindergarten were compared with a control group of 550 who did not attend preschool but did participate in all-day kindergarten. This study is the most comprehensive review of a widely recognized and respected large-scale program. It supports findings found in the earlier Perry Pre-School (Michigan) and Abecedarian (North Carolina) studies.

A 2002 cost benefit analysis of the Chicago CPC pre-K program found $47,759 in net present value benefits and $6,692 in net present value costs in 1998 dollars, or a benefit to cost ratio of 7.1 to 1.

Converting these results to an annual return on investment suggests long term results to the non-participating public and government at least comparable to the 12% ROI derived by Rolnick and Grunewald (Federal Reserve Bank of Minneapolis) in their 2003 evaluation of the Perry preschool program.

Sponsors of the program attribute its success to a number of critical factors.

Language-based instructional programming is diverse and structured to promote social and academic success. High priority is given to recognition of letters and numbers, oral communication, listening and an appreciation for reading and drawing. Child-to-teacher ratios in pre-K (17 to 1) and kindergarten (25 to 1) are low, promoting individualized and intensive learning. Under the supervision of the "parent-resource teacher" the parent program is comprehensive involving classroom volunteering, attendance at school events and educational courses for personal development. A "school-community representative" coordinates resource mobilization, home visitation and location and enrollment of children most in need.There is continual staff development for all personnel at each center. Special services are provided, including health screening, speech therapy, shared nursing services and free breakfasts and lunches.

In contrast to many preschool programs, teachers in the CPC program have at least a bachelor's degree with certification in early childhood education. Staff stability and compensation are high relative to other programs. Individual classrooms have one teacher's aide and often parent volunteers. Each center includes a parent-resource teacher who implements programs for parents in the "parent resource room." Children generally enter the program at age three for a three-hour morning or afternoon session during the regular nine-month school calendar. CPC programs operate under the sponsorship of the Chicago Public School system in a wing of the elementary school or in a separate building close by. A head teacher manages each center coordinating child education programs, parent involvement, community outreach, health and nutrition.

CALCULATING THE RETURN ON INVESTMENT

The methodology used by Reynolds and Temple to calculate the rate of return on the initial dollars invested in the program was based on the most comprehensive analysis of an established large-scale program yet undertaken. Pre-kindergarten students had relatively higher rates of educational achievement as well as attainment of health insurance, lower rates of the more serious criminal behaviors such as felony arrests, convictions and imprisonment and lower rates of depressive symptoms. Reynolds and Temple 2007 19-year follow-up study was the first to recognize the linkage between quality pre-K participation and higher rates of insurance coverage and lower rates of depressive symptoms, likely a result of higher school achievement. Since expenditures for medical care and criminal justice system represent about 20% of GDP, the prospective cost savings to taxpayers are large.

Educational attainment data was derived from school records and a survey of participants or family members. Criminal justice system involvement was obtained from governmental agencies plus an adult survey. Economic wellbeing was assessed from the Illinois Department of Employment Security as well as the adult survey. Health insurance data came from both public (Medicaid) and private (employer-based) sources. Depressive symptoms were reported in the adult survey.

In the 2002 study Reynolds and his colleagues identified $47,759 in net present value benefits and $ 6,692 in net present value costs in 1998 dollars.

The benefits derived primarily from lower public education costs due to lower grade retention and special education, reduced costs in the criminal justice system and for victims due to lower crime rates, greater earning power by center participants and increased tax revenue reflecting higher lifetime earnings of program participants. Not included in the computation of the 7.1 to 1 benefit to cost ratio were the benefits derived from reduced pain and suffering by victims. Also the prospective savings from lower welfare usage on the part of center participants was not evaluated. Finally, the benefit to the next generation by parents who adopted healthy life styles could not be calculated.

Benefits of the Chicago-Parent Center Pre K Program

	Non-Program Group	Program Group
Special Education by age 18	24.6%	13.6%
Grade Retention age 15	38.4%	23.0%
Years in Special Education (from ages 6-18)	1.43	.73
Arrested by age 18	25.1%	16.9%
Arrested for Violent Offenses (by age 18)	15.3%	9.0%
High School Graduation (age 20)	38.5%	49.7%
Have Insurance Coverage (age 24)	61.5%	70.2%
Victim of Abuse or Neglect (ages 4-17)	10.3%	5.0%
Full time Employment (age 24)	36.4%	42.7%

Source: Reynolds et al (2002/2007)

THE ECONOMICS OF INVESTING IN UNIVERSAL PRESCHOOL EDUCATION IN CALIFORNIA

A recent California study reveals the documented results to society from high quality early childhood educational programs. Published in 2005 by the RAND Corporation it is entitled, "The Economics of Investing in Universal Preschool Education in California."

The RAND Corporation used data compiled over thirty years in a longitudinal study conducted by the Chicago based Child Parent Centers (CPC) program. RAND used this data base because the results fell midway between the outcomes generated by other longitudinal studies including the Perry Preschool project and the Tennessee based Early Training Project. California demographics, economic status and ethnic profiles for children were then applied to the CPC data base.

Total benefits to California Society were estimated to approximate $11,400 per participating child. This number was offset by costs of $4,339 per child to provide a gain of $7,036 per child in net benefits. This computes to a total return on investment of 162% or an internal rate of return for California society of 10.3% over a sixty year time horizon from the initial preschool investment.

THE CALIFORNIA UNIVERSAL PRESCHOOL PROGRAM

- *Voluntary program for all age-eligible children.*
- *The program enrolls 4-year-olds.*
- *It involves 525 hours per year of intensive program activity.*
- *"Wraparound" care is available with extended-day care financed by other sources.*

- The maximum class size is 20. The staff-child ratio is 1-10.
- The head teacher in each classroom has a bachelor's level education with an early childhood education credential. The assistant teacher in each classroom has an associate's level degree.
- Programs use existing or new facilities run by both public and private providers.
- Public dollars fully fund the programs.

California adjusted the 30-year experience of the Chicago Child Parent Centers (CPC) program to reflect its own demographic and preschool experience. The statistical results for like programs were then used by California to determine the value added from intensive preschool training for 4-year-olds. The CPC Program has tracked children from age 4 to age 21 and 22. The statistically significant results include:

- Advantages in reading achievement scores as late as age 14.
- Lower likelihood of retention in grade by age 15.
- Reduced use of special education through age 18.
- Lower incidence of child abuse and neglect from ages 4-17.
- Lower likelihood of involvement in the criminal justice system by age 18.
- Greater likelihood of high school graduation by age 20.

CALCULATING THE RETURN ON INVESTMENT

To calculate the costs of a universal program assumptions are made about the hours per day involved, the weeks per year, class room space required, staffing needs both teaching and administrative and wage rates. The resulting total is about $5,700 per child. Estimated current spending is deducted to arrive at the net cost per child figure of $4,379.

- Educational savings come from the reduction in grade repetition and decrease in years spent in special education. The increase in high school graduation rate also triggers an estimated offsetting cost in higher education costs as college attendance increases.
- Savings from reduced child welfare expenses come from savings to government and victims related to lower rates of child abuse and neglect. Case histories are used to determine the costs related to physical injuries and mental health issues.
- Identifiable costs are used to determine savings to government and victims of crimes processed through the juvenile justice system. Estimates of the cost of adult crime can be linked to the reduction in juvenile crime.
- With respect to compensation and the impact on taxes the CPC program tracked differences between those attending preschool and those who did not. Lifetime earnings to age 65 were assumed.
- The value of child care was estimated to equal the hourly rate of the minimum wage with the assumption that hours spent in day care would free up an equivalent amount of time for employment.

BENEFITS (COSTS) TO SOCIETY

Source	California* $/Child	California* $/Cohort(mm)	U.S.Total* $/Child	U.S.Total* $/Cohort(mm)
Program Cost	-4,339	-1,671	-4,339	1,671
Program Benefits				
Education Outcomes	876	337	992	382
Child Welfare	102	39	141	54
Juvenile Crime	1,220	47	1,220	470
Value of Child Car	2,406	926	2,406	926
Total Measured	4,604	1,772	4,759	1,832
College Attendance	-173	-67	-173	-67
Employment	5,801	2,234	7,940	3,057
Adult Crime	1,143	440	1.143	40
Total Projected	6,772	2,607	8,910	3,430
Total Benefits	11,375	4,379	13,669	5,262
Net Benefits	**$7,036**	**$2,709**	**$9,329**	**$3,592**
Benefit-Cost Ratio	2.62		3.15	
Internal Rate of Return	10.3%		11.2%	

* Amounts are in 2003 dollars and reflect the present value of amounts over time where future values are discounted to age 3 of the participating child. Dollars per cohort assume a cohort of 4-year-olds of 550,000 children and a 70% pre–school participation rate. Source: page xxix of "The Economics of Investing in Universal Preschool Education in California" published by the RAND Corporation.

CRITIQUE

It would be helpful to have available additional longitudinal studies representing greater geographic and ethnic diversity. Fortunately, the tracking of results in the previous studies was performed over long time periods by objective evaluators. One can certainly ask why every state hasn't established long-term measurement systems since the quality of life experience for a child and the impact the child has on society can be tracked back to the initial years of life. A child undergoes significant growth and change up to about five years of age. The available data is convincing that high-quality pre-school programs for children in poverty can enhance educational performance, contribute to their economic benefit, reduce anti-social behavior and provide a high return on taxpayer investment. While the data may show some fading in intellectual advantage after age 7, later general literacy, school achievement, reading, language and arithmetic subtests show strong advantages for the program groups. Educators believe that the enhanced caring atmosphere and social interaction with the program groups contributed to growth in non-cognitive areas of the brain that enhanced life time learning and behavior.

Improving High School Graduation Rates with the Quantum Opportunities Program

In the USA about 75% or more of the adult prison inmate population did not complete high school according to state departments of corrections. There is a higher correlation between dropping out of school and ending up in prison than there is between smoking and lung cancer. In most states high school dropouts earn at a maximum 66% less than those who graduate. Considerable evidence now exists to prove that incentives can increase the odds of a student graduating from high-school. The Minneapolis-based Wallin Foundation has provided college scholarships to more than 3,000 students who have met rigorous academic standards and graduated from high school. On going mentoring is an essential part of the process both in high school and later in college.

"Quantum Opportunity" is a four year-after-school, weekend, and/or summer program for ninth through twelfth graders in high-crime and high-poverty neighborhoods. It is comprised of small groups of up to 25 students with a youth leader. Students spend up to 750 hours each year beyond normal class time in basic educational programs, personal skill development and community service. There is a funded scholarship "Opportunity Account" for either post-secondary education or vocational training. The cost of $2,500 per student per year includes the program expense and the scholarship account.

The program was developed by Opportunities Industrialization Centers of America, Inc. It is a youth development program for socio-economically disadvantaged youth with the goal of improving academic performance. The original demonstration program enlisted 25 students at each of five different sites in the USA: San Antonio, Philadelphia, Milwaukee, Oklahoma City and Saginaw, Michigan. Students were entering the ninth grade and from families on welfare. Initially 76% were African American, 11% Hispanic, Asian or other ethnic origin and 13% were

White. At each site 50 ninth grade students were randomly selected from families on public assistance, and then one-half were assigned to QOP directors with the balance comprising the control group.

A questionnaire gathered information on demographics, work experience, school history, health data, personal attitudes and opinions. Also academic levels (vocabulary, reading comprehension, mechanics, computation, concepts and expression) as well as functional skill levels (knowledge of occupations, economics, government, health and community resources) became part of the data base. The tests used were the Test of Adult Basic Education and the Comprehensive Competencies Program (CCP) Tier Mastery. These were repeated in 1990, 1991 and 1993.

KEY FINDINGS

By the end of the second year the average test scores for program participants was much higher in five of eleven academic and functional areas (vocabulary, comprehension, mathematics, computation, mathematics concepts and language expression). By the end of the forth year, average group scores were higher in all of the eleven areas.

Where boys and girls participated in the program, juvenile crime was reduced by 56% and adult crime by 50%. Boys not in the program were found to be six more times likely to be convicted of a crime. Boys and girls who did not participate in the program were 50% more likely to have children during the high school years. Youth who did not participate in the program were twice as likely to dropout of school.

The 125 youth who participated in the initial pilot program were far more likely to graduate from high school (63% vs. 42%). Youth who participated in the program were 2.5 times more likely to go on to further education or training after high-school.

It also found that per dollar spent QOP was over five times more effective at preventing serious crime than the Three Strikes Law in California. Each $1.00 spent prevents over 250 serious crimes.

CALCULATING THE RETURN ON INVESTMENT

- *It is assumed that the life long cost of dropping out of high school approaches $300,000 (lower tax revenues, higher cash and in-kind transfer costs, and imposed incarceration costs) relative to an* *average high school graduate. A graduate with four years of college adds nearly $800,000 in value to taxpayers versus a dropout.*

- *The total cost of the program over four years is estimated to be $12,000.*

- *Test data revealed that 21% of the 125 participants were more likely to graduate from high-school*

21% X 125 = 26 participants more likely to graduate from high school

26 X $300,000 = $7,800,000 of total opportunity savings

125 X $12,000 = $1,500,000 of total program expense

$7,800,000/$1,500,000 = $5.20 returned for each $1.00 invested or a net taxpayer gain of $4.20 per dollar of expense.

CRITIQUE

With the type of results noted above one wonders why more notice hasn't been given to the QOP program. The opportunity exists for local and national foundations to take the lead and survey existing QOP programs to determine where the opportunity for expansion exists both locally and nationally. Expanded tracking of selective programs could reinforce the earlier positive return on investment conclusions as well as promote best practices which it turn could be applied throughout our secondary school educational systems.

Sources: RAND, "Diverting Children from a Life of Crime: Measuring Costs and Benefits," 1996; Robert Taggert, "Quantum Opportunities Program," Philadelphia: OICA, 1995; Fight Crime: Invest in Kids, "America's After School Choice: The Prime Time for Juvenile Crime, or Youth Enrichment and Achievement," 2000; Hahn, A., T. Leavitt and P. Aaron, Evaluation of the Quantum Opportunities Program, Heller Graduate School, Center for Human Resources, Brandeis University, Waltham, Mass., 1994; Lattimore, C. Benjamin, The Quantum Opportunities Program, Blueprints for Violence Prevention Series, Book 4, Center for the Study and Prevention of Violence, Institute of Behavioral Science, University of Colorado at Boulder, 1998.

Curing Child Abuse and Neglect with Targeted Home Visitation Programs

The National Institute of Justice has found that children who are abused or neglected are 53% more likely to be arrested as a juvenile, 38% more likely to be arrested as an adult (77% more likely if female) and 38% more likely to be arrested for a violent crime. In Hennepin County, Minnesota, a study in 2000 showed that more than 14,000 calls were received about suspected child maltreatment, 5,550 calls were investigated by a case worker, and in more than 2,600 cases, abuse or neglect was substantiated. In Minnesota, 11,113 children were determined to be abused or neglected in a 1999 study. Physical abuse totaled 2,727 cases, sexual abuse 802, neglect 8,021, and mental injury 109.

Minnesota's Department of Health targeted home visiting programs are specifically designed to prevent the neglect and abuse of children. The program sends trained public health nurses that visit at risk families for several hours each month to observe behavior, recommend positive in-home helpful practices and, where appropriate, connect the family with other resources. These services are offered before and after birth on a voluntary basis to families who meet established risk criteria. Families are connected with primary health care providers and community based services by public health nurses who make direct calls on the targeted home. The objective is to promote positive parenting skills and eliminate practices harmful to the development of healthy children.

A pilot program in Minnesota's Faribault and Martin Counties showed that only 3% of children in the target population experienced substantial maltreatment versus an estimated 20% maltreatment rate for kids not in the target group. Indiana's "Healthy Families Initiative" had a success rate of 99% with only 10 out of 1,026 families found to confirm abuse or neglect at 15 sites statewide. In Hawaii's "Healthy Start" program 99.9% of families were free of abuse or neglect at 12 sites statewide. Arizona's "Healthy Families" project experienced a 97% success rate.

CALCULATING THE RETURN ON INVESTMENT

Child protection systems generally have been crisis-driven with little opportunity to implement preventive techniques. Most serious offenders evidence anti-social behavior as early as pre-school age. Preventing anti-social behavior has a direct correlation with the prevention of juvenile crime. Home visiting through public health nurses costs between $1,500 and $4,000 per family annually. The estimated average cost of hospitalization for an abused child for one week is $9,000. Juvenile detention centers cost over $50,000 for one year of treatment. Adolescents whose families received services at least ten years in the past are 55% less likely to be arrested, 80% less likely to be convicted of a crime, 60% less likely to run away and less likely to use alcohol, drugs and tobacco during adolescence.* In addition welfare expense is reduced and family stability and earnings potential are enhanced.

One of the more comprehensive cost/benefit studies relating to the benefit of targeted home visitation programs was conducted by the Brookings Institution in 2003.** Studies were conducted in three cities (Elmira, Memphis & Denver) for infants age 0 to 2 who received home visits by a public health nurse over a two and one-half year period. For infants at high risk in Elmira the average program cost of $7,300 yielded benefits estimated at $41,000 for a cost benefit ratio of 5.68. For low risk infants the cost benefit ratio was 1.26.

The three city study for both high and low risk infants had an average cost of $9,000 resulting in benefits of $26,000 for a cost benefit ratio of 2.88 or an equivalent ROI of 188%.

For most states with large budget shortfalls, the highest priority should be to preserve spending that produces the greatest payoff for the taxpayer. Focusing on infants believed to be at high risk surely qualifies. It produces a net benefit of more than $4.00 for each dollar invested.

CRITIQUE

A continuing challenge in the field of child abuse and neglect is often the reluctance of an adult present to immediately report the event. In

---

*Prenatal and early Childhood Nurse Home Visitation, U.S. Department of Justice, Juvenile Justice Belletin, November 1998.

**Brookings Institution, "Cost Effective Investments in Children/ Nurse Family Partnership for First Time Mothers" 2003.

most cases the abuse or neglect is repetitive. As quality pre kindergarten centers evolve in greater numbers observed evidence and reporting of abuse should improve. Pre and post natal education programs must also be more available for families. The economic return on home visitation is high and it warrants an aggressive effort by local municipal and county officials to insure that neighborhoods, with strong evidence of abuse or neglect, be targeted for high impact special programming. This could take the form of an integrated awareness program for church, education, business and other civic leaders to have access to a coordinated abuse or neglect reporting system. Local government officials should also be required to report annually the number of qualified home visitation staff present, relative to the number of suspected abuse and neglect incidents reported, to insure sufficient qualified staff are employed.

Mortgage Foreclosure Prevention Programs Can Be Highly Cost-Effective

Foreclosure prevention programs generally work as follows: Community based organizations provide direct counseling and information on options available to homeowners who typically are four to five payments behind on their mortgage after an average of seven years of successful performance. Screening is conducted to ensure that financial problems result from circumstances beyond the family's control: health problems, job loss, large extraordinary expenses, divorce or death of a spouse. The homeowner's financial problems must be solvable, and the homeowner must be willing to work with the program staff to develop and follow a plan to resolve these problems. Emergency financial assistance may be provided to assist the homeowner in becoming current on the mortgage. Intervention and advocacy is provided, such as negotiation with the mortgage servicer or lender.

The benefits of well-managed foreclosure prevention programs are many. Families benefit because foreclosure results in the loss of a secure place to live, a loss on average of $7,200 invested in the home (1993-1995 dollars), a damaged credit rating and likely higher costs to replace the home through purchase or rental. Taxpayers benefit from avoiding the potential loss of real estate and sales tax revenues and possible increase in social service program expense when families are displaced from their home. State and local government and therefore taxpayers benefit by avoiding the write off of investments in neighborhoods providing affordable workforce housing. Neighborhoods suffer image and vandalism problems when properties are boarded-up. Banks and other mortgage lenders, mortgage servicing companies and mortgage insurance companies benefit from not having to write off direct investments, lose interest payment income and not having to incur expenses related to holding and maintaining properties in default. The federal government (HUD) and therefore taxpayers benefit by avoiding costly write-offs of FHA and VA insured loans and the attendant processing expenses.

Based on a four year study completed in 1995 by the "Family Housing Fund" of Minneapolis, Minnesota, by the end of the second year after mortgage foreclosure counseling was conducted experience indicates a 180% return on investment to private "financial sector" investors and a 360% return to "federal, state and local government" investors.

Because the Family Housing Fund "Mortgage Foreclosure Study" covered the period from 7/1/91 to 3/31/95 the numbers used in calculating the returns are in 1993-1995 dollars. The foreclosure study surveyed over 800 families in Minneapolis and St.Paul. Nearly 60% of homeowners (487) who received counseling and/or emergency assistance had their mortgages reinstated. Fifty percent of the "reinstated" homeowners (244) were current after two years in the program. Total prevention expenditures were $1.6 million or $3,300 per homeowner served or $6,600 per homeowner still current after the second year. While there is a drop off in homeowners surveyed current on their mortgages after the first year experts in the field believe that delinquencies stabilize at the end of the second year. Estimated expenses if a property moves all the way through the foreclosure process are as follows:

FORECLOSURE COST PER PROPERTY (FHA INSURED MORTGAGES)*

FHA-HUD	$26,500
The City	27,000
Neighbors	10,000
Homeowner	7,200
Lender	1,500
Servicer	1,100
Average Cost Per Foreclosed Property	$73,300

*Reflects costs when foreclosure runs the full course.

FORECLOSURE COST PER PROPERTY (PRIVATELY INSURED MORTGAGES)*

Private Mortgage Insurer	$16,000
Homeowner	7,200
Lender	2,300
Servicer	1,100
Average Cost per Foreclosed Property	$26,600

*Assumes property is put on the market and sold recovering some foreclosure expense.

CALCULATING THE RETURN ON INVESTMENT

FACTS: Prevention expenditures were $3,300 & $6,600 respectively per homeowner for years one and two of the program.

ASSUMPTIONS:

Direct Value to Government of Prevention	Year 1	Year 2
Benefit to FHA & HUD	$26,500	$15,000
Benefit to State & City	27,000	15,200
Total Benefit Per Foreclosure Avoided	**$53,500**	**$30,200**

Direct Value to Private Insurer or Mortgage Lender	Year 1	Year 2
Private mortgage insurance or direct write-off of loan	$16,000	$15,200[†]
Lender and/or loan servicer expense	3,300	3,100
Total Benefit Per Foreclosure Avoided	**$19,300**	**$18,300**

*Reflects fact that 56% of mortgages surveyed are current in the second year. Also the savings shown are less than the example displayed previously since foreclosure has not had to run the full course.

†Foreclosed properties sold in year one. Year two number simply reflects the present value at 5%.

The Resulting ROI to Government & Private Investors

$30,200/$6,600 results in second year ROI to government of nearly 360% or ($4.57 for each $1.00 invested).

$18,300/$6,600 results in second year ROI to private investors of nearly 180% or ($2.77 for each $1.00 invested).

Critique

The Family Housing Fund Study of November 1995 has been used to measure the cost effectiveness of Mortgage Foreclosure Prevention. The losses incurred only reflect direct costs for the property involved excluding staff expenses and other administrative costs. While the study used in this example is not as current as one would wish, it was conducted during a period of more normal real estate valuation. The value added by foreclosure avoidance counseling may have increased further after the recent real estate bubble and subsequent decline in values. Clearly in recent years the avoidance counseling system has been overwhelmed. An updated study would add credibility to what appears to be a very high ROI program for the public as well as the private and public investors directly involved.

Supportive Transitional Housing Can Move Individuals from Welfare to Work

Supportive transitional housing is defined as that step in the housing continuum that moves individuals and families from homelessness to semi-permanent housing, with the expectation that eventually the individual and family will achieve a permanent solution to their housing needs and become self-sufficient. Nearly 60% of those in shelters are people of color, about 50% have some degree of mental illness and about one third were abused as kids. The majority of women in shelters have fled an abusive relationship. When youth wind up on the street homeless, nearly 50% become compromised by drugs, crime or sexual exploitation after 24 hours. Nearly one third of these youth have considered suicide and more than one-half have been sexually molested. Since 1991 the number of youth in shelters has tripled!

The research shows that there are multiple benefits from well-managed supportive housing programs that provide effective support services. The individual and their family benefit from taking that significant first step on the road back to safety and self-sufficiency. The re-acquired feeling of self-worth and identification with someone who cares become powerful positive motivators towards eventual self-sufficiency. The community benefits as healthy families find the type of shelter with supportive services that promotes greater stability at home, in the neighborhoods, in our schools and at the workplace. Ultimately, the taxpayer benefits from programs that initially require added investment, but offer the high probability that longer-term social service support costs will decline and personal incomes and tax receipts will rise.

Bob Wagner, former director of outreach at the The Church of Saint Stephen of Minneapolis put it this way, "When one is homeless one has no sense of self or place and a complete inability to solve problems. There is a total lack of identity with no self-esteem. Having a place to sleep and subsequent work assessment testing is the first step in recovering a sense of self-worth and feeling that...someone out there cares."

127

The Minnesota Supportive Housing & Managed Care Pilot*

In March 2009 a group of individuals averaging five years of homelessness were divided into two groups, one receiving standard services and the other intensive case management, including help accessing benefits, health care, life skills development, financial literacy training and aid restoring family relationships. While the cost of services for the two groups was nearly the same, the mix of services changed dramatically from maintenance support to services that clearly advanced the opportunity for self-sufficiency. It was clear that the most expensive group when comparing the pilot program people with the others were single adults, with cost differences dramatically lower for family adults and children.

In general, the pilot group experienced reduced costs for prison/jail, mental health outpatient services, chemical dependency inpatient, detox and medical inpatient. The cost structure shifted in favor of child welfare, income support, medical outpatient, mental health outpatient and pharmacy. The key result of the pilot program was greatly improved housing stability, with participants spending 144 out of 180 days in their home compared with pre-program numbers of 64 days at home out of 180. Participants were better able to handle complex challenges and also have their location known to social workers, friends and family.

The Hennepin County Supportive Housing Study

The results of this study completed by Hennepin County (comprises the greater part of the Twin Cities metropolitan area) in July 2003 show that while there is a modest gain in the total public cost when an individual moves from homelessness to transitional housing, that the odds improve dramatically for that individual to ultimately achieve self-sufficiency. What happens is that the composition of the public investment changes dramatically in favor of services that promote healthier long-term life styles as opposed to emergency help that offers no lasting benefit. The question the study asked was, "Does supportive housing reduce residents' use of county crisis services, and does the overall service usage of residents show a shift towards long-term stability?" Twenty-nine families

---

*This study was funded by the Robert Wood Johnson Foundation, Route 1& College Road East, PO Box 2316, Princeton, NJ 08543-2316......www.reif.org.

who lived at Portland Village in south Minneapolis during its first year of providing supportive housing were the basis for the study.

Using what are believed to be conservative assumptions a return of 18% on the original investment was earned after ten years. It is likely that even higher returns would be earned in future years as stable housing with services increases the number of people working and reduces even further social service and criminal justice system costs.

Crisis intervention costs for homeless individuals and families include: treatment for substance abuse, a range of child protection services and the expenses incurred from out of home placement of children. These costs decline significantly where supportive housing is provided over a 12-month period. It is interesting to note that a relatively small number of families account for better than half of the total crisis intervention costs of this study.

Supportive prevention services are investments in the future of the family and they include: child care assistance, early childhood services, developmental disability support, services aimed at preventing entry into the child protection system, adolescent parent support and mental health services. These costs generally rise with intensive case management since they contribute to a child's stability, health and development.

Economic assistance payments by the federal and state governments rise as residents achieve stability and greater awareness and access to the assistance that is available. These payments include federal support such as food stamps and general assistance as well as Minnesota Supplemental Assistance and MFIP (Minnesota Family Investment Program). There was a dramatic decline in out-of-home placement for children from 2,433 days prior to the children moving into supportive housing to 336 days while living at Portland Village. This allowed many children to be reunified with their parents and others to experience new foster care arrangements. Two adults spent nearly the entire year in the state or county women's correctional facility immediately prior to moving into Portland Village. The cost of incarceration totaled $67,500. While living in supportive housing, two adults spent only one day each in a county jail. Supportive housing provided a home for them to return to, while focusing on rehabilitation as well as a safe and supportive place for their children.

Calculating the Return on Investment

The Hennepin County study of July 2003 documents 29 families who resided at the Portland Village residential facility for twelve months. The comparison is made between county, state and federal government costs for the twelve months preceding Portland Village residency and the cost incurred for the twelve months at the residency.

Prior to residence at Portland Village, federal and state governments spent $265,176 per year on these families. Hennepin County spent $261,321 per year on these families with 78% of the cost being crisis services and only 22% being supportive services. While at Portland Village total costs for these families rose to $372,184 but crisis services comprised only 17% of the total cost while supportive services and housing comprised 83%. This change in emphasis towards self-improvement services together with the stability provided by safe housing increases the odds that a number of these families will achieve self-sufficiency within five years.

If we assume that 15 of these families will achieve self-sufficiency five years after arriving at Portland Village with earning power of $10.00/hour, we can conclude that there will be a savings over a 10-year period to the county, state and nation of $1,489,333 from the $5,264,970 that would have been spent had these families remained homeless. The savings reflects reduced county crisis expense and lower federal and state welfare payments (MFIP, Emergency Assistance, Food Stamps etc.) Since the county, state and nation invested a total of $1,265,695 in Portland Village-related supportive services and payments, the net savings from the total investment in the Portland Village program is $223,635 or a 18% return over the 10- year period on the initial investment ($223,635/$1,265,695).

Facts:

Henn. Co. Cost per Year for 29 Families Pre Portland Village	$261,321
USA & MN Cost per Year for 29 Families Pre Portland Village	$265,176
Henn. Co. Annual New Investment for 29 Portland Village Families	$110,863
USA & MN Annual New Investment for 29 Portland Village Families	$59,856

Assumptions:

- 14 families will remain at Portland Village for 10 years with no improvement.

- 15 families have earning power of $10/hour after 5 years and exit Portland Village.
- State and Federal Tax receipts remain constant at $53,700 (sales and income taxes).
- County, State and Federal benefits and services will remain constant for ten years.

Ten Year Cost/benefit Analysis

Hennepin County Crisis & Supportive Costs Pre Portland Village
$2,613,210
USA & Minnesota Welfare Support Costs Pre Portland Village
$2,651,760
$5,264,970 **Total prospective cost of 29 homeless families for ten years**

Hennepin County New Investment in PV:

$535,220	14 families for ten yrs.
$286,715	15 families for five yrs.

USA & Minnesota New Support Costs in PV:

$288,960	14 families for ten yrs.
$154,800	15 families for five yrs.

$1,265,695 Total New Investment in Portland Village.

Savings from 15 families taken off of County ($675,830) and
State & USA ($685,800) support after five years
$1,361,630
Savings from 2 individuals avoiding nine months of prison time
$75,000
Federal & State tax receipts from 15 families earning $10/hour for five years (sales and income tax)
$53,700

$1,489,330 Total estimated benefit from Hennepin County Investment in Portland Village.

$223,635 Total Net Benefit (Savings of $1,489,330 less net public investment of $1,265,695).

Favorable cost benefit of $1.18 for each $1.00 invested

Critique

A key enhancement would be a longitudinal study that tracks these families after the initial year at Portland Village or like transitional housing facilities. A number of studies track the change in composition of supportive services that increase the odds of individuals and families moving towards self-sufficiency. However, funds have yet to be allocated for tracking future progress. One would assume that this data is accessible from county, state and federal information systems. Pressure on government budgets continues to place performance tracking systems too low on priority lists.

Section Three

The Art of Changing and Improving Public Policy

A review of how six leading workforce development non-profit organizations, two leading philanthropic organizations, a few creative state employees and a couple of interested citizens created a new system for measuring the effectiveness of federal and state job skill training programs.

The advantages of being well connected to one's community are often unexpected. I was reminded of that truth a few years ago after I had completed several initial return-on-investment studies that were published in "An Investment Letter for Minnesota Philanthropists." That periodic newsletter drew on experiences derived both in my investment career and in service my wife and I devoted over the years to non-profit organizations. It was distributed to the more than 1,000 members of Minnesota's "One Percent Club," which promotes charitable giving from net worth, and to publicly elected officials in state and local government. One such official, Mike Christenson, heads planning and economic development for the city of Minneapolis. Mike was interested in moving the Minneapolis City Council towards a more active role in job skill training and workforce development. I was asked to present to the Minneapolis City Council my findings about the positive economic returns to the community generated by individuals who had completed training from several of our leading non-profit organizations.

The presentation appeared to go well, and the council found additional resources to devote to both year-round and special summertime employment programs. Their move reflected a growing understanding of economic development's vital contribution to urban vitality. Christenson, together with his colleagues in Minneapolis and Hennepin County, awarded job skill training contracts to numerous non-profit organizations in the region.

The resulting city/county job training network has evolved over time because of the skill and insight of leaders such as Roger Hale, retired CEO of Tennant Company; Mike Brinda and Deb Bahr-Helgen at the city of Minneapolis and Chip Wells with Hennepin County.

After several successful years, Christenson thought that the program had sustained such a strong track record that the State of Minnesota's Department of Employment and Economic Development (DEED) should be made aware of its training techniques and evaluation methods. A meeting was arranged with the DEED commissioner and his staff at the Minnesota workforce center on east Lake Street in south Minneapolis. Christenson began the presentation with an overview of Minneapolis's successful history in attracting unemployed and underemployed individuals to its job skill training program. He followed with data that illustrated how these organizations were evaluated, how contracts from the city were put out for competitive bids and then awarded on a basis of merit. I then illustrated how over time, the training costs incurred by these non-profit organizations were not only recovered in a short period of time, but thereafter contributed a very positive economic return to the community and the taxpayer. I thought this would give DEED a strong case for requesting additional funding for job training programs from the Legislature. The commissioner and his staff asked a few questions about our methodology, but for the most part their reaction to our presentation was polite but underwhelming.

I pointed out that my efforts to evaluate and demonstrate success were handicapped by the lack of a measurement system that allowed the State of Minnesota to track whether graduates of these programs were still working in Minnesota, in what industries, and at what wage. I suggested that developing that capacity was in taxpayers' interest. After all, I noted, the state passes federal dollars through to the cities and counties, which in turn fund these programs. In addition, the state directly pays for Minnesota's own workforce training system. I mentioned that most non-profit training programs cannot afford to track the careers of their graduates for more than one year after completion of the program. I knew of only one that was able to track after two years.

The state should develop a system to track program graduates for five to ten years, I recommended. Do this successfully, I argued, and you will be able to show the taxpayer why these programs are a good investment, and will attract more funding from the Legislature. Further, this type of evaluation system would allow the state to determine which programs best serve individuals with varying training needs. Alignment of job training programs with Minnesota's higher education system would also be enhanced. We concluded the meeting cordially but with no apparent commitment by the commissioner to pursue these recommendations further. (In subsequent years, former Minnesota DEED commissioner Dan McElroy took considerable interest in collecting and monitoring job training results).

As I walked down the hallway of the workforce center, I felt a tug on my coat sleeve. One of the commissioner's assistants, Libby Starling, said, "Mr. Heegaard, I believe we have a computer system that with some enhancements might be able to pull together the data you want." What followed was one of the most productive luncheon meetings I have ever had. We met at Biaggio, a small restaurant in the midway district of St. Paul. Libby Starling asked me what exactly I wanted to know.

It would be helpful to be able to track the earnings, past and future, for graduates of the various workforce training centers, I said. This would be possible, she said, but for confidentiality purposes, these data could only be disclosed in clusters of three individuals or more. I asked if it would be possible to release the average wages of a cluster of trainees. She said yes, and also indicated that they could in addition calculate the mean of the group's wages. I asked if the data could indicate the federal code for the industry in which the individuals worked. This would certainly be possible, she said. I knew this information would help align training programs to those industries in which their graduates found employment, and to the higher education institutions in which some training program grads enrolled.

Encouraged, I plowed ahead: Could the state tell us the nature of a graduate's work, such as accounting, marketing, manufacturing or service? To my surprise, she responded, "No, only the state of Alaska compiles that type of data." Her knowledge of what other states were doing impressed me. The problem, she said, is while the data I wanted are available in various state information systems, the issue of confidentiality impedes their release. Further, existing computer programs would not extract the data I sought in a format that would be useful. Budgetary constraints apparently had prevented the development of an information system up to this task.

My mind shifted gears. If enough funds could be generated from the foundation community, I asked, could we hire under the state's auspices a programmer who could write the software needed to generate the results I sought? She saw no reason why this wouldn't be possible. We parted with Libby Starling expressing her willingness to continue to be helpful, and my commitment to present this opportunity to friends in the foundation community.

Getting respected local foundations involved in my data quest could be beneficial in several ways, I soon realized. Given the skepticism many citizens have about government's ability to manage programs well, bringing private sector expertise to bear on the evaluation of government programs would add credibility to the effort. Further, if foundations could be sold on the longer-term positive economic returns to taxpayers from well-managed workforce training programs, it logically followed that funds might be made available to help prove this case to legislators, who authorize the funding for the great bulk of the state's employment programs. For foundations, it would be a way of substantially leveraging their investment in programs with a high return to taxpayers and to the state's economy, which in turn would be viewed positively by the foundation's donor base.

Shortly after my meeting with Libby Starling, I was called to a meeting with Frank Forsberg and Marcia Fink at the Greater Twin Cities United Way. They wanted to learn more about the work that several of us had been doing in attempting to calculate the return on investment to the community from selected well managed non-profit organizations. I told them my intent was to demonstrate a methodology for calculating the return on investment by certain non-profits. I was a rookie at this exercise, I explained. I hoped a more sophisticated organization could build on my work documenting more precisely the benefits derived from investing in non-profits.

Some months after this meeting, I received a call from Luke Weisberg, a well-known Twin Cities-based economic development consultant and former director for the Governor's Workforce Development Council. Luke indicated that he had been retained by the Greater Twin Cities United Way to review the Minneapolis/Hennepin County workforce training organizations I had been examining, with the goal of trying to sort out which organizations were doing the best job. He had worked closely with Libby Starling and others at DEED, and was fully aware of the limitations in the state's ability to evaluate the public's investments in these programs. With Luke's confirmation that an investment to improve the state's evaluation capability made sense, I approached colleagues at the North Star Fund, affiliated with the Minneapolis Foundation. They expressed enough interest to warrant a gathering of interested parties.

On July 26, 2006, the group that would become the initiators of this public/private partnership met at the Minneapolis Foundation. It included Paul Anton, a research economist with Amherst H. Wilder Foundation, Luke Weisberg, Debra Serum of DEED, Libby Starling by then with The Minnesota Housing Finance Agency, Eric Anderson, Joanne Walz, and Marigrace Deters of the Minneapolis Foundation and North Star Fund advisors Bridget Hust, Libby Carrier Doran, Donald Brown and myself.

The group agreed on two goals:

1. Accessing the State of Minnesota's DEED database to mine relevant data for ROI measurement of nonprofit employment training programs.

2. Assuming significant and positive ROI results, using that information to advocate for reallocation—and/or increase of—state and federal funding to non-profit employment training programs. This data might in addition influence and increase foundation, corporate, and individual fundraising by non-profit organizations.

We learned that day that state government had all the likely necessary information in its various databases with the exception of jobs outside of the workers compensation system. "Return on Investment" eventually could become part of a new and revised state reporting system, we were told. It would cost about $75,000 annually for DEED to employ a person with the qualifications to manage this program. Nobody flinched at that amount.

The next meeting, on September 28, 2006, pulled together the original key stakeholders, including Marcia Fink of the Greater Twin Cities United Way, plus the CEOs of the largest Twin Cities non-profit training programs. These included Mike Bingham of Twin Cities RISE, Louis King of Summit Academy OIC, Jane Samargia of HIRED, Steve Studt of Project for Pride in Living and Michael Wirth-Davis of Goodwill/Easter Seals. We confirmed those organizations' ability to provide the necessary information on individuals and cohort groups that successfully completed training and were placed in jobs. Greater Twin Cities United Way would be the lead financial partner in the data mining project, with the balance of the funding provided by the North Star Fund of the Minneapolis Foundation. DEED would be the third partner in the venture with project coordination provided by Luke Weisberg. It was also recognized that funding might be required for a five-year period.

It was agreed that two major projects would be pursued. The first was to develop a real-time, forward-looking tracking effort to obtain wage information for cohorts (groups ranging in size from 10 to 25) of participants in workforce development programs. This required training providers to obtain releases from program participants to allow wage records to be used to track their future employment. Next these non-profits would have to provide participant names and/or Social Security numbers, formatted as prescribed by DEED. The DEED staff would shoulder responsibility for explaining the necessary formats and reporting back to the service providers and funders as required.

The second project would establish 'baseline" data, looking back 3-5 years to evaluate the value of past workforce training by the five major providers. This would provide a basis for comparison later when new data became available. This would involve gathering program records, formatting data consistent with DEED's requirements, and reporting frequently to all stakeholders so that any needed adjustments in data or formatting could be made in a timely manner.

With that game plan set, the hard work commenced. We not only had to conduct an in-depth analysis of the state's various databases, but also had to work our way around the legal and ethical obstacles involved in extracting private information about graduates of Minnesota's workforce training programs. Staff had to be hired and contracts developed between the various funding parties and DEED. In addition, the workforce training centers had to adopt DEED's formatting requirements and direct their own limited personnel to engage in additional paper work.

It was slow going, but by the end of 2008, considerable progress had been made. Project coordinator Weisberg reported early in 2009 that both the forward-looking tracking capability and the baseline data collection were nearing completion. In March, Weisberg announced that the data collected from Greater Twin Cities United Way workforce center grant recipients from 2003 to 2007 had been applied to an initial methodology for computing return on investment. It revealed that the average placement rate for trainees was just over 65 percent, with 15 percent off the payrolls after three months. The net placement rate was about 50 percent. Average earnings increased about $5,000 the first year for all participants. The information also revealed that individuals with severe barriers to work (immigrants/public assistance recipients/medical issues) were significantly aided by timely interventions by programs sponsors.

By mid-2009, we were doing a test analysis of data obtained about the most recent graduates of the workforce programs. From this very preliminary data the initial ROI calculations were made: the average earnings increase for trainees immediately after completing the program was $4,000, compared with an average cost per trainee of about $3,900. These public investments were achieving break-even status in the first year, even before future enhanced earning power is assumed, taxes paid are calculated and the benefit of reduced social service and criminal justice system costs are factored into the equation. When those things are eventually factored into the ROI formula, the "investors" (elected officials, government department heads, foundation executives, philanthropists and non-profit managers, to name a few) should see a more positive trend line on investment returns.

I've taken away from this experience a number of lessons. One is that a few citizens can have considerable impact when they spot an unmet need or opportunity, and have the patience and determination to search for a way to address it. Next, organizations such as the United Way and North Star Fund of the Minneapolis Foundation are critical providers of financing and expertise to citizens who step forward with a worthy idea for improving the shared life of the community. The willingness of the training centers themselves to take on the burden of data collection without immediate financial reward was absolutely crucial to our effort. Their public spirit is a community asset.

But at a time when public employees are too often faulted even by the politicians who aspire to be their bosses, I must salute the true heroes of this story: the DEED employees. They were able to step back from their own day-to-day tasks and see merit in a project that would create more work for themselves. Libby Starling had the courage to speak out and to then follow through with her colleagues to define exactly what needed to be done. Finally the skill, patience and vision of our consultant Luke Weisberg was essential to the success of this effort, which expanded in scope and complexity as it evolved.

With funding for this project committed through 2011, the results of "The Return on Investment Workforce Study" will soon be made available to a much broader constituency. The technology developed for this purpose ought to find wider application, not only with workforce training providers but also with other government and non-profit activities. A number of states have sponsored ROI analyses of programs dealing with early childhood education, K-12 and higher education, the criminal justice system, housing, health care and family services, to name but a few. In would appear to be of benefit to taxpayers to insist that all major governmental units add such assessments to their work. A modest initial investment can produce the information government needs to deliver on political promises of "more bang for the buck."

Section Four

ROI Use by Nationally Acclaimed Research Institutes

I'm far from alone in seeking a way to consistently and credibly measure the return on investments in non-profit organizations. National research organizations are also engaged in this work, often as an outgrowth of their analysis of public policy options for clients including government, charitable foundations and individuals. They've made considerable progress toward establishing the standard methodology for evaluating non-profit performance that I believe ought to now emerge.

Several of the non-profit agency ROI studies in Section 1 rely upon the work performed by these professional research-based organizations. This section reviews the work of several of them, with supporting detail found in the appendices. I am grateful to the Wilder Foundation, which has a history of performing in-depth analysis on a range of public policy issues and which hosted a national conference of several of these research organizations in July 2008. There, nationally recognized speakers applied ROI metrics to entities whose missions include education, criminal justice and juvenile justice as well as workforce training.

WILDER FOUNDATION:
"Measuring Your Program's Financial Benefits"

In this study, Paul Anton, when serving as a research scientist for the Wilder Foundation, illustrates how non-profit organizations can more effectively tell their story with the use of return-on-investment calculations about their key programs. This process is often called cost-benefit analysis or the computation of the social return on investment (SROI). It has had extensive use in Europe and is a logical expansion of current applications of program evaluation. The study explains that while program evaluation responds to the question: Does program X work?" ROI analysis answers the question: Is it worth it that program X works?"

Recent Wilder ROI studies have been conducted on drug courts, youth mentoring programs, supportive housing, methamphetamine treatment programs and welfare to work programs. In Minnesota applications of ROI methodology are under way by the Greater Twin Cities United Way, Governor's Workforce Development Council and the Minnesota Department of Employment and Economic Development. Nationally the John D. and Catherine T. MacArthur Foundation has initiated a $35 million grant program called "Measuring Social Benefits." The newly formed Benefit Society of America promotes joint work in the field of ROI analysis between academics and practitioners. Finally, Anton recommends a new book, *Investing in the Disadvantaged*, by David L. Weimer and Aiden R. Vining (Georgetown University Press, 2009.) It summarizes the state of current analysis in fields such as education, healthcare for the disadvantaged, juvenile crime, encouraging work and numerous others.

A step-by-step guide for the application of ROI analysis by non-profit organizations is highlighted in Appendix 1. To be relevant, Anton says the work must result in decisions whether to keep an existing program, modify it or replace it with something more cost-effective. He also notes that ROI analyses are useful for demonstrating value, allocating resources, promoting accountability and engaging stakeholders. He provides an understandable and useful description of the differences between a benefit-cost ratio, net present value and the internal rate of return.

Current economic conditions have increased demands by funders for information about "results," Anton notes. As a result, non-profit organizations themselves are seeing an increased need for more reliable data on which to base decisions. Anton maintains that the economic contributions of non-profits to their communities have often been underrated. ROI studies can help better illustrate their true value for both today and the future.

For more information contact: Wilder Research, Paul Mattessich, Executive Director, 651-280-2700, or *research@wilder.org.*

WASHINGTON STATE INSTITUTE FOR PUBLIC POLICY
"Building Bi-Partisan Support for Public Policy Initiatives"

The Washington State Legislature created its own think tank in 1983 with the mission of "carrying out non-partisan research on projects assigned by the legislature or the Institute's board of directors." Based at the state capital in Olympia, the center's recent work has dealt with prevention programs in early childhood, K-12 education outcomes, child abuse and out of home placement of children, substance abuse and mental health, developmental disabilities and crime, criminal justice costs and prison construction.

Washington state lawmakers routinely invite the Institute to inform it before they make a major policy move. For example, the Institute's recent early childhood assignment from the legislature was to "review research assessing the effectiveness of prevention and early intervention programs...to reduce at-risk behaviors for children and youth...and identify specific research-proven programs that produce a positive return on the dollar compared to the costs of the program." In the area of education the challenge was "to study the cost-benefits of various K-12 educational programs and services. The goal for this effort is to provide policymakers with additional information to aid in decision making." Legislative directives for other studies can be found in Appendix 2.

The evaluation process for these projects involved, first, an assessment of whether enhancements to an established process could be identified; next, if a cost-benefit analysis of those enhancements could be made; and finally, whether state policy changes occurred, or were advisable. The study of developmental disability was made too early in the process of change for results to be determined. But each of the other recent studies was able to conduct cost-benefit analyses of enhancements to existing processes, and to offer either recommendations for legislative action, or to identify legislative action that had contributed to positive results.

The value of cost-benefit analysis was clearly evident in the work done to improve Washington state educational outcomes. The research noted a steady rise in the state's high-school graduation rate from 1870 until about 1970, when it reached 78 percent, and then a gradual decline to 74 percent in 2004. Concern over this finding triggered research to evaluate a number of possible policy changes, including the cost-benefit of reducing average class sizes.

One study was aimed at the economics of lowering class size for kindergartners. First, the operating and capital costs required to cut class sizes or fund full-day versus half-day kindergarten were determined. Then, on the benefit side, an estimate was made of the lifetime labor market gains and cost benefits (lower health care, crime, foster care) coming from gains in K-12 test scores and graduation rates. The return on investment numbers could then be calculated. The results were based upon 38 statistically sound studies (including 69 separate grade-level tests) of the impact of class size reductions on K-12 test-score outcomes.

The results showed substantial improvement in test scores for grades K-2, more modest but positive gains in grades 3-6 and little to no improvement in middle and high school. The findings showed that a one-unit drop in class size costs about $220 per student (operating and amortized capital costs.) For K-1 the return on investment was 8.3 percent (range 5.7 to 11 percent) and for grades 3 through 6 the ROI was 6 percent with middle school and high-school having negative returns. An additional finding based on economic profiles showed that low-income students benefited the most from reductions in class size.

The Institute has conducted a variety other K-12 studies, including several pertaining to the cost-effectiveness of improvements in teacher compensation, training, certification and performance incentives.

The Institute has also put cost-benefit analysis to good use in examining state corrections and crime-reduction policies. It found substantial per-person advantages (benefits less costs) for incarcerated adults in vocational education, intensive supervision of inmates in treatment-oriented programs, general education, cognitive-behavioral therapy and community-based drug addiction treatment. Gains were also evident with programs such as drug treatment in prison, adult drug courts, employment and job training in the community and electronic monitoring to offset jail time.

Of interest was the finding that while sex offender treatment in prison with aftercare reduced negative outcomes 7%, it had a negative cost benefit of about $3,000. That finding raised a question that the numbers alone cannot answer: When is a small gain worth pursuing, even at high cost?

The Institute has found more positive ROIs associated with juvenile offender programs. Multidimensional treatment foster care ($78,000 net benefit), adolescent diversion project, family integrated transitions, functional family therapy on probation, multi-systemic therapy and aggression replacement training all were shown to be worthwhile financially. Other programs with positive returns included: juvenile boot camp to offset institution time, sex offender cognitive behavioral treatment, restorative justice for low-risk offenders, interagency coordination programs and juvenile drug courts. But the Institute found negative cost-benefit ratios in juvenile intensive probation supervision programs and regular surveillance-oriented parole. While a program entitled counseling and psychotherapy for juvenile offenders showed a 19 percent reduction in outcomes it also broke even in terms of cost benefit analysis.

For additional information on the work of the Washington State Institute for Public Policy contact Steve Aos, Assistant Director.
E-mail: saos@wsipp.wa.gov / Phone: 360-568-2740
Institute Publications: *www.wsipp.wa.gov.*

THE PEW CENTER ON THE STATES:

"Advocate for Non-partisan, Pragmatic State Policy Solutions to Critical Problems Facing Americans"

The Pew Center on the States, a department of the Pew Charitable Trusts, responds to the critical need states face to restructure priorities and redesign programs so that budgets can be balanced while maintaining the highest priority services. PCS forecasts that total currently mandated federal spending programs will exhaust all federal funding resources by 2029 (See Appendix 3). PCS advocates a new approach to state and federal budgeting that "increases the value placed on long-term interests, evaluates economic returns, subjects all areas of the budget to comparable treatment in the budget process and regularly compares new and existing funding opportunities." It urges governments to anticipate demographic changes and respond to changing demands for health care, education, corrections, retiree pensions and infrastructure.

Appendix 3 details one example of Pew's work: its study of corrections reform in Kansas. Since the annual per-inmate cost of incarceration in state facilities averages at least $50,000, even a small reduction in the number of inmates can render considerable savings.

Pew's 2007 study in Kansas found that former offenders comprised 65 percent of all prison admissions. Goals were established to reduce probation revocations by 20 percent, at an estimated added cost to taxpayers of $4.5 million. This required an analysis and employment of the best practices for reducing revocations by certain high-risk offenders. Once those practices were in place, their continued funding was made contingent on good performance by corrections officials in the field. As illustrated in Appendix 3, the new plan delayed the need for additional prison space in the state to 2018, versus a previous estimate that added capacity would be needed by 2009. In other words, a prison population expected to increase by 22 percent in the next decade is now projected to stay almost flat.

For additional information contact The Pew Center on the States, 901 E Streert NW (10th floor), Washington DC 2004-1409; 202-552-2000; www.pewcenterforthestates.org ; Susan K. Urahn, Managing Director; s.urahn@pewtrusts.com

BROOKINGS INSTITUTION:

"Cost-Effective Investments in Children"

In a series of Brookings Institution research papers examining ways of balancing the federal budget over a five-year time period, a 2008 study by Julia B. Isaacs stands out. (The complete series can be found at *www.brookings.edu/budget*.) Isaacs performs a cost-benefit review of four areas of investment that she argues deserve increased federal funding "even in a time of fiscal austerity." The study is comprehensive and detailed in terms of the factors that go into the cost-benefit analysis. While she does not convert the ratios derived to ROI equivalents, in most cases the duration or time frame is included so that rough ROI computations can be made. The four areas of investment she examines:

1 **High-quality early childhood education programs for three- and four-year-old children;**
2 **Nurse home visitation programs to promote sound prenatal care and healthy development of infants and toddlers;**
3 **School reform with an emphasis on programs in high-poverty elementary schools that improve the acquisition of basic skills for all students; and**
4 **Programs that reduce the incidence of teenage pregnancy.**

Isaacs examined programs with each of these four goals and converted the cost/benefit conclusions into return per dollar invested. In other words, a concluding number of 2.50 means that $1.00 invested generates $2.50 of return. To convert this to a return-on-investment equivalent requires deducting the initial $1.00 program investment return from the final result, providing an ROI of 150 percent for the stated time period.

Her early childhood education analysis of four programs found clear positive returns ranging from 2.56 to at least 7.14. She divided the savings by category—criminal justice, taxes, education, welfare, child welfare, and other government—for each of the four programs. These comprise estimated savings to government. She then added an estimate of savings to society through a reduction in crime and increase in family earnings. That distinction may be helpful to future policymakers.

Isaacs' findings have considerable potential to guide both government policymakers and non-profit administrators. For example, she found that the value of nurses visiting first-time parents is greatest when nurses visit families deemed "high risk," such as a teenaged single parent. In addition to calculating favorable benefit cost ratios ranging from 1.26 to 5.68 among the highest risk families, Isaacs found that home visitation programs delayed the time between first and subsequent births, resulted in more appropriate play materials for kids and resulted in less punishment of children.

Based on her findings, Isaacs endorses a $2.9 billion enriched program for children in elementary school that uses time-tested approaches to ensure that all children acquire basic reading skills. Isaacs reminds us that one-third of the nation's fourth grade kids do not perform at a basic reading level, with an additional gap (one-half not performing) between poor and minority children and their peers. She points out that "one study of the long term effects of Head Start found that children in Head Start often enroll in poor quality schools after the program, possibly explaining why IQ gains due to Head Start participation fade out more quickly for black children than for white children." Three studies are reviewed with benefit cost ratios ranging from 1.00 to 7.14 with the best results from a program that focuses on ages 3 and 4 and the next best from one serving ages 6 to 9.

Many programs attempting to prevent "Teen Pregnancy" have not been proven to be highly effective. Issacs highlights two that have had positive results. Both emphasize a range of efforts with youth development as opposed to a more narrow focus on sexuality. Of the two, the "Teen Outreach Program" places even less emphasis on family planning and more on sound decision making, social competence in dealing with adults and skill in handling ones own emotions. The cost-benefit analysis shows results ranging from .21 to 1.29. Those numbers may be understated. The possible impact of the programs on juvenile delinquency or employment after high school was not measured, nor was the benefit to the community of the programs' "service learning" component.

For more information about the Brookings Institution and the study on "Cost-Effective Investment in Children" contact Julia B. Isaacs at Brookings in Washington D.C.; 202-797-6000 or *www.brookings.edu.*

URBAN INSTITUTE JUSTICE POLICY CENTER:
"Return on Investments in Crime Control"

The Urban Institute conducts non-partisan research on a broad range of topics that affect national, state and local governments. With the total cost to American society of major crimes exceeding $350 billion per year, crime control ranks among government's most important work and its best opportunities for "more bang."

John Roman's Urban Institute study applying ROI to crime control assessed the cost-benefit factors associated with drug courts, services to prisoners reentering society, and using DNA evidence in property crimes. Since spending on crime control continues to grow faster than inflation as prison population rise, Roman argues that ROI analyses can lead to greater efficiency in crime control efforts.

Roman offers convincing evidence that court mandated drug treatment can cut crime rates by 10-20 percent, compared with non-treatment incarceration. Despite several studies with similar conclusions, less than 5 percent of people arrested in the United States enter a treatment program. As a result, he concludes, the use of special-purpose "drug courts" to mandate treatment might currently reduce crime by no more than one-half of one percent. However, he says, if all criminal justice clients currently eligible to be treated by drug courts were enrolled in treatment while incarcerated, the national savings would exceed $32 billion annually. Roman identifies the problem as "scarce financial resources by government and risk-aversion by prosecutors and defense attorneys."

Roman examined Maryland's Reentry Partnership Initiative (REP), which provides case management services for state inmates during incarceration and for two years following release. REP's regimen includes substance abuse treatment, mental and physical health treatment, education programs, job readiness and employment, housing and family/community reunification assistance. A comparison study of 229 REP clients with 370 non-REP prisoners showed a reduction in recidivism, 72 percent from 78 percent, and 68 fewer crimes committed by REP participants. The conclusion was that REP yielded about $3.00 in benefits for every dollar in new costs, for a total benefit of $21,500 per REP participant.

Roman's work also confirmed the value of collecting DNA evidence, comparing it with traditional investigative techniques. It proved superior in identifying suspects, arrest rates and cases being accepted for prosecution. What makes a ROI calculation challenging in this instance is that more effective use of DNA costs government about $25,000 per case. While its benefit accrues to citizens and society in general and likely well exceeds the cost, in the near term it may not result in immediate savings to taxpayers. In these cases Roman suggests that a system of internal government agency credits could be applied to reward a department for external benefits whose costs cannot immediately be offset by anticipated future savings.

For more information about the Justice Policy Center "Return on Investment" study contact the Urban Institute: *www.urban.org* or Justice Policy Center: jpc.urban.org or John Roman: jroman@urban.org.

University of Texas Ray Marshall Center:
"Workforce ROI Estimates"

The study performed at the university's school of public affairs expanded the concept of return on investment to compute estimated benefits from workforce training separately for program graduates, taxpayers and society in general. Based on data gathered between 2003 and 2005 by the state's workforce centers, the analysis provides annualized internal rates of return as well as conventional ROI measures for program participants entering both high and low intensity jobs.

If anything, the Marshall Center study may underestimate the value of the programs it examines. That's because it makes no attempt to evaluate reductions in spending by state and local support programs and the correctional system as result of workforce training. It considers only program graduates' wages earned and taxes paid five and ten years after program completion, as well as the elimination of federally sponsored welfare support payments. It pegs the program's costs to foregone participant earnings plus direct program expenses.

Nevertheless, the study calculated a highly attractive ROI. Returns from the program after five years per dollar invested were 3.6 for society in general, 3.9 for taxpayers (government) and 4.6 for the participants themselves. After ten years, returns per dollar invested were larger: 6.2 for society, 6.7 for taxpayers and 7.8 for participants. At both five- and ten-year intervals, internal rates of return were exceedingly high relative to nearly all other benchmarks, ranging from a low of 86 percent to a high of 116 percent.

The Ray Marshall study concludes that well-run workforce services pay substantial dividends. It adds that while both low and high intensity services lead to substantial returns, the benefits that derive from high-intensity services are greater and more enduring.

For more information about the Workforce ROI report from the Ray Marshall Center at the LBJ School of Public Affairs at the University of Texas at Austin contact Christopher T. King, director; or *ctking@uts.* *cc.utexas.edu* ; Phone: 512-471-2186
Web Site: *www.utexas.edu/research/cshr.*

MACALESTER COLLEGE:

"Estimating the Economic Benefits of National Workforce Training Programs," by Robertson, Hottman & Berman

This study (detailed in Appendix 4) combines the research skill of two Macalester College professors of economics with the executive experience of workforce training program CEO Arthur Berman. It provides a comprehensive analysis of the many variables that go into assessing the ROI of workforce training programs. Its database is national in scope with current data collected for each of the 50 states and the District of Columbia. The authors are candid in describing the unknowns that require many assumptions to be made when analyzing the economic benefits of training programs. For example, in the absence of a comparative longitudinal study, one cannot be certain of the number of months an individual spent receiving government income assistance prior to training, nor how much more such assistance a trainee could have received. Guesswork about that variable is required in calculating the gains that result when government income assistance is no longer needed by program graduates. Eight different sets of assumptions are made in the study.

The Macalester study concludes that government investment in workforce training is justified. In addition, the authors point out that the economic gains to workers and their employers justify their own investment in these programs. The payoff to government and taxpayers can be huge, especially when considering the present value of welfare (TANF) and criminal justice system savings along with federal and state taxes collected over a ten-year period of gainful employment. The study also found substantial variation in benefits from workforce training among the 50 states.

Notably, this study refers to another factor that is often overlooked when analyzing workforce training's benefit—the multiplier effect on economic activity from spending by new wage earners. The authors also make a distinction between portable skills that all employers want their workers to have and specialized skills unique to a particular job. Naturally, most employers prefer not to train workers in the basics, since those skills can be applied across many industries. That is one reason the authors advocate a role for government not just in investing in quality training programs but also in basic education, including student aid support.

"Current expenditure per trainee may be less than optimal," the authors conclude. "On a simple cost/benefit basis, more training would be beneficial, and...training workers may also benefit children and future generations." (The authors have applied their metrics to the Twin Cities RISE! case study included in Section One.)

For additional information contact professor Raymond Robinson at Macalester College, 1600 Grand Avenue, St Paul, Minnesota 55105 or *robinson@macalester.edu.*

CENTER FOR LABOR MARKET STUDIES, NORTHEASTERN UNIVERSITY:

"U.S. Teen Employment the Lowest Ever Recorded in Post-World War II History"

Today's very high rate of youth unemployment was addressed in a presentation by Andrew Sum at the May 2009 National Association of Workforce Development Professionals conference in Minneapolis. Sum is employed by the Center for Labor Market Studies at Northeastern

University. Sum reported that the U.S. teen employment-to-population ratio was then a mere 29.8 percent, the lowest recorded in post-World War II history. By comparison, the ratio was 45.2 percent in 2000. Importantly, Sum noted that in all years, males, low-income youth, youth of color and high school dropouts fared worse than average. It is surprising to many that middle- and upper-income youth are employed at much greater rates than lower-income youth. For example, for African American youth with annual family incomes below $20,000, the employment-to-population ratio in March 2009 was just 12 percent. During the same time period, the employment-to-population ratio of white youth with family incomes of $75,000 - $100,000 was 35.7 percent.

Sum projected that the average high school dropout will cost taxpayers through a lifetime more than $292,000 in lower tax revenues, higher cash and in-kind transfer costs, and incarceration costs relative to an average high school graduate. In contrast, a graduate with four years of college adds nearly $800,000 in value to taxpayers.

Sum cited many reasons to engage disadvantaged youth in the local labor market.

- Employment for economically disadvantaged males while in school, especially blacks and Hispanics, increases their high school graduation rate.
- In-school employment with work-based learning opportunities increases students' awareness of the links between high school curriculum and the world of work requirements; it can increase commitment to school work and strengthen employability skills.
- Working while in high school improves the transition to the labor market upon graduation from high school, producing higher employment rates and earnings.
- Local areas characterized by higher employment rates for teenaged girls have lower teen pregnancy rates.
- Local labor markets with higher employment rates and wages for boys also see lower incidence of juvenile crime, particularly assault/battery, and property crimes.
- Work reduces the attraction of drug sales among inner city youth.

Sum's assertions have been affirmed by other researchers. "Studies show a direct benefit of early work experience for teens," wrote Linda Harris of the Center for Law and Social Policy in her 2005 article, "What's a

Youngster to Do? The Education and Labor Market Plight of Youth in High Poverty Communities." Harris concluded: "Work experience in the junior or senior year of high school adds to wages in the later teen years and to increased annual earnings through age 26, especially for those not attending four-year colleges. Youngsters in high-poverty communities are disadvantaged by their lack of early work exposure during the critical years when they should be building their labor market attachment, their workplace skills, and a portfolio of experiences that would allow them to progress."

For additional information contact Andrew Sum, Director The Center for Labor Market Studies, Northeastern University, 315 Homes Hall, 360 Huntington Avenue, Boston, MA 02115. Email: a.sum@neu.edu. For publications: *www.clms.neu.edu.*

Conclusions and Recommendations

Cost/benefit analysis is an emerging and potentially powerful tool that deserves to be more widely employed by government and non-profit organizations. As the case studies in this book illustrate, it has the potential to steer policymakers to make wiser choices, even as it inspires greater confidence among donors and taxpayers that their money is being spent well. It is the essential first step to the zero based budgeting process that some states are adopting as they re-set priorities in attempting to close large budget deficits.

I'm convinced that the non-profit organizations and entrepreneurs I examined with this tool are delivering "more bang for the buck." When a combination of private and public support has allowed them to develop expertise, they have moved the social and economic health of their communities forward. Where leadership skills are apparent and the basic management tools of planning, organizing, staffing, communicating and evaluation are employed, results are generally very good. Where they are not, a market not unlike the private sector's causes them to either improve or disappear.

But cost/benefit analysis, long familiar to business investors, is still in its infancy in the non-profit and government realms. My review leads me to offer these recommendations for realizing the full potential of cost/benefit analysis:

1. More accurate, uniform, widely recognized and reported measures of program effectiveness are needed. Currently, the reporting of methodology and results is too varied and incomplete. Too often it requires anyone attempting analysis to make far too many assumptions about data relating to costs and benefits. Institutions of higher education can make a significant contribution to this effort by part-

nering with non-profit organizations, as illustrated in Appendix 4, to develop standards.

2. Greater commitment to transparency by both government and non-profit organizations is key. I commend the St. Paul, Minnesota-based Charities Review Council for its method of urging greater transparency in non-profit reporting: It has established "Standards of Accountability" and each year, it singles out for public recognition those organizations that either partially or fully meet those standards. Key among its standards is "public disclosure, " that is, legal compliance/financial reporting, listing of accomplishments and reporting consistency. This kind of encouragement can help an organization evolve its data collection and accounting practices in a way that makes cost/benefit analyis easier.

3. For cost/benefit analysis to have credibility, it must be objective, understandable and presented by managers of the highest quality. The surfeit of information of varying reliability available at the click of a computer mouse today gives the quality of management and accuracy of the data they present even greater significance than they have in the past. The need to base public policy on solid data means that leaders must devote an increasing share of their own time and talent to new ways of gathering, analyzing and communicating the right kind of information.

4. Not every worthwhile public endeavor can or should be converted to an ROI formula. For example, ours is a society that cares for its disadvantaged citizens. This is an American core value. Therefore, citizens and elected officials must apply their best qualitative thinking when it comes to the allocation of resources for those challenged with physical, mental and emotional issues. We also highly value human rights, safe communities, access to a fair judicial system and a host of other core values that do not easily lend themselves to cost/benefit analysis.

5. Non-profit organizations should see cost/benefit reporting not as a replacement for the qualitative reporting to their constituencies they already do, but as an enhancement of it. Managers that honestly set forth the facts, state clearly any necessary assumptions and display the math they use to reach return-on-investment conclusions will enhance their organizations' marketing appeal, while bringing valuable discipline to their evaluation processes.

Clearly there is an opportunity for non-profits that demonstrate strong cost/benefit ratios to play a larger role as government subcontractors than they have in the past. In these days of tight public money and recurring political gridlock, employing apolitical non-profits with their cadre of volunteers seems like an obvious way to get public work accomplished.

Governments increasingly are applying cost/benefit analyses to their oversight of the partnerships they establish with the private and non-profit sectors. While I welcome that development, I'm concerned that governmental funding strictures are often so tight that they don't allow enough resources for effective evaluation. For example, if the Minnesota Department of Human Services could update annually the information required in Appendix 5, far more effective reviews could be conducted, helping to improve the effectiveness of our income support and workforce training programs.

In addition, when cost/benefit analysis is done by government funders, it may take place so far up the political food chain that the credibility of the data that's collected is suspect by either the left or the right. Washington State's Institute for Public Policy avoids that problem by offering evidence-based input early in the legislative process, before the political battles emerge. That makes good sense. The Institute's study on the impact of reducing student/teacher ratios is a case in point.

Government bureaucracies are notorious for collecting data for one narrow purpose and not recognizing its wider utility. The example cited in Section Three illustrates the point. The objective information needed to measure the effectiveness of federally and state funded workforce programs already existed in various state data bases. However, it had not been extracted in a format that was meaningful to anyone. Thanks to a process initiated by citizens, government staffers, foundation leaders and non-profit managers, a revised system is now in place. It allows Minnesota's executive branch to demonstrate to legislators and taxpayers that its workforce development programs are cost effective and save taxpayers money over time.

My hope is that cost/benefit analysis can eventually reduce the credibility gap that exists between taxpayers and their government. While traditional debates between the left, center and right will always be with us, mistrust and disbelief have swelled and are impeding America's ability to solve problems.

The tax bills citizens receive offer little information about how their tax money will be spent or what benefits might be gained from that spending. Categories such as "tax increment district" mean little to an average citizen.

There is no reason why a report could not accompany tax statements that describes spending categories that comprises five percent or more of a governmental unit's budget, and explains the benefits expected to be derived from that spending and the number of people served.. The same data could be offered online and updated more frequently than annually, so that it is readily available to citizens and those who seek to represent them in elective office.

If cost/benefit analysis became part of the debate over the size and role of government, the quality of political discourse could improve. Taxpayers are used to hearing government spending described as an investment, but they are understandably suspicious when the term is used without creditable documentation. A credible analysis of the return on investment produced by public spending could reduce waste and at the same time document those programs for taxpayers where government spending has a future payoff that justifies some sacrifice today.

M innesota once had a State Planning Agency to guide policymaking. If such an agency were revived, it could be an ideal administrative home for compiling and synthesizing cost/benefit analyses by municipal, county, special purpose district, state and federal units of government. It could assure that the analyses were easily accessible.

Foundations too have expanded their use of cost/benefit analysis. These organizations, in concert with leading think tanks such as those listed in Section Four, can do much to advance the tool's wider use. For example, government is prone to responding to a program that demonstrates a high return on investment with "Yes, but. . ." Yes, but we have short-term fiscal constraints, and cannot afford to budget for the longer term benefits. Yes, but the political system is so focused on the short term that elected officials can't risk spending now to save later. What if the philanthropic community were to say, "Let us fund a pool of resources that will pay for this program's expenses, and then let us be reimbursed over time from the cost savings it eventually produces." They would be offering to provide a "prove it to me" vehicle, one that would require a partnership between the philanthropic community and government that would extend five years or longer. If it succeeded, it could inspire more confidence among taxpayers and voters that government can effectively spend now to save later.

Foundations could also work in partnership with appropriate levels of government to support and strengthen the management of non-profits that tackle some of our toughest community issues. Clearly, more support is needed for those attempting to provide youth employment, curb neighborhood violence, stop predatory lending, provide high-quality pre-K education and secure adequate transportation for urban workers to suburban jobs. Given the right data, foundations can better target their efforts at enhancing non-profit effectiveness, by improving management systems, consolidating or partnering with other non-profits and implementing their own cost/benefit oriented performance review process.

The effectiveness of the things a democratic society chooses to do in concert ought to be every citizen's concern. That's why I urge every citizen to push governments and non-profit organizations to more fully measure and report the cost/benefit ratios of their endeavors. Return-on-investment considerations should be among the questions put to all candidates for public office. In fact, one might argue that public policies won't improve until voters adopt this practice.

It may be satisfying to blow off steam and hurl invectives at this policy or that candidate, but in a democracy, griping shouldn't pass for constructive citizenship. Complaining can be a very expensive pastime. But if citizens join together in groups and apply the same energy to candid debate over policy, informed by objective knowledge of a range of possible costs and resulting benefits, the result could be a major transformation of American government for the better. There's enormous opportunity for progress in citizens simply knowing what works best and together being determined to get more bang for their buck!

Appendix 1

RETURN-ON-INVESTMENT:
MEASURING YOUR PROGRAM'S FINANCIAL
BENEFITS

Paul Anton, Wilder Research
Evaluation workshop: September 11, 2009

PURPOSES OF THIS WORKSHOP

- Introduction and overview of the technique of ROI analysis

- Understanding of its growing use in the human services field

- Practical guidance for your organization on if and how to use such analysis

AN OUTSTANDING EXAMPLE

High Scope/Perry Preschool
From 1962-1967, 3- and 4-year-old African American children in Ypsilanti, Michigan

- Randomly chosen and assigned to a high-quality early child-hood education program

- Participants were contacted at intervals and interviewed

- 97% still alive and interviewed at age 40

Figure 1: Major Findings of the High/Scope Perry Preschool Project for Participants Followed Up at Age 27

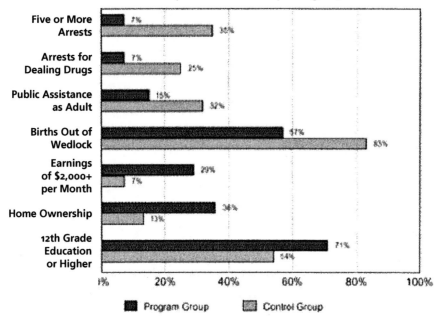

Source: HighScope Educational Research Foundation. 1999 High-Quality Preschool Program Found to Improve Adult Status. Yipsilanti MI. HighScope Educational Research Foundation.

ROI CALCULATION

Total value of benefits	$108,200
Total cost of program	$12,356
Estimated return on $1 invested	$8.74
Estimated % return	16% per year

Source: Rolnick and Grunewald, Early Childhood Development: Economic Development with a High Public Return

Return-on-investment analysis

- Also called benefit-cost analysis, sometimes social return-on-investment (SROI)

- A well-established tool in economics and policy analysis

- Used extensively in Europe; growing use in US

- A natural extension of program evaluation

Relation to program evaluation

- Program evaluation answers the question:
  "Does program X work?"

- ROI answers the question:
  "Is it worth it that program X works?"

— By comparing the costs of the program with the dollar value of the benefits it produces

Growing use of ROI

At Wilder Research

- Recent and ongoing studies include:
  Drug courts, youth mentoring programs, supportive housing, methamphetamine treatment programs, and welfare-to-work programs

- 2008 conference included
  speakers on Education, criminal justice and juvenile justice, manpower training programs

IN MINNESOTA

- Greater Twin Cities United Way
  Preparing ROI analyses of all manpower training grantees

- Governor's Workforce Development Council
  Task force to set standards for ROI analyses of workforce programs

- Minnesota Department of Employment and Economic Development
  Legislative mandate to produce ROI analysis of all programs

IN THE UNITED STATES

- John D. and Catherine T. MacArthur Foundation
  "Measuring Social Benefits" –a $35 million grant program

- Benefit-Cost Society of America
  Formed in 2008 to foster development of the filed and joint work between academics and practitioners

- Book: Investing in the Disadvantaged, *edited by Weimer and Vining*

  Summarizes state of analysis in a number of fields including education, healthcare for the disadvantaged, substance abuse, juvenile crime, encouraging work, and others

STEPS IN RETURN-ON-INVESTMENT ANALYSIS

1. Measure the total cost of a program

2. Measure the outcomes produced by the program

3. Estimate benefits by valuing the outcomes in dollars

4. Compare the dollar benefits to the dollar costs

5. Clearly identify the alternative for comparison

   - No treatment or program
   - Alternative existing treatment
   - Previously existing program
   - If new, the program it will replace

1. MEASURE TOTAL COST

Direct expenses (payroll, administrative expenses, materials, etc.)
Imputed expenses (incl. depreciation and interest foregone, parent program participation (if any))
Donations (incl. volunteers time)

2. MEASURE PROGRAM OUTCOMES

Formal program evaluation outcomes, plus
Any other social or economic effects of program versus "no program"
Note: All outcomes must be differential effects between program and alternative

3. Value Program Outcomes

- Translate non-monetary outcomes into dollar values using

Market analogues

Social science research

Economic reasoning

- Usually the most challenging step

- Often not all outcomes are measurable or monetizable

Example: Estimating the benefits of reducing truancy by an average of one day per student

100 Students in youth intervention program

1.8% Increase in high school graduation rate

1.8 Additional high school graduates

---

x $263,000.00

    Present value of after-tax earnings
    differential for a high school grad

$473,400.00 total value of after-tax earnings

$4,734 Per student benefit of reducing student truancy by one day

4. COMPARE BENEFITS AND COSTS

- Benefit-cost ratio: "X dollars for every dollar invested"
  Net present value: "Total value of X dollars"

- Internal rate of return: "X percent return on dollars invested"
  –(similar to the interest rate on a bond)

USING RETURN ON INVESTMENT

USES

- Demonstrating value
- Making decisions
- Allocating resources
- Promoting accountability
- Engaging stakeholders

USERS

- Program staff and Management
- Board of Directors
- Donors
- Public Officials
- Grant-making Foundation Executives

WHY USE ROI ANALYSIS?

- Increasing demands by funders for information about "results"

- Nonprofit organizations feeling greater need for information to make better decisions

- Nonprofit organizations have been slighted –their worth has been undervalued

Appendix 2

WASHINGTON STATE INSTITUTE FOR PUBLIC POLICY:

(CREATED BY THE 1983 WASHINGTON LEGISLATURE)

MISSION: CARRY OUT NON-PARTISAN RESEARCH ON PROJECTS ASSIGNED BY THE LEGISLATURE OR THE INSTITUTE'S BOARD OF DIRECTORS

Overview	**Directions**	E.g., K–12	Cost Benefit	Bottom Line

Recent Legislative Directions to WSIPP to Produce Cost-Benefit and Evidence–Based Information:

Prevention Programs in Early Childhood (2003 Session)
"...review research assessing the effectiveness of prevention and early intervention programs...to reduce the at-risk behaviors for children and youth...and identify specific research-proven programs that produce a positive return on the dollar compared to the costs of the program."

K-12 Education Outcomes (2006 Session)
Study "the cost-benefits of various K–12 educational programs and services. The goal for the effort is to provide policymakers with additional information to aid in decision making. ."

K-12 Education Outcomes (2007 Session)
Develop funding options that "...reflect the most effective instructional strategies and service delivery models and be based on research-proven education programs and activities with demonstrated cost benefits."

Child Abuse and Out of Home Placement of Children (2007 Session)
"...study evidence-based, cost-effective programs and policies to reduce the likelihood of children entering and remaining in the child welfare system, including both prevention and intervention programs."

(Continued) Recent Legislative Directions to WSIPP:

Substance Abuse and Mental Health (2005 Session)

"...study the net short-run and long-run fiscal savings to state and local governments of implementing evidence-based treatment of chemical dependency disorders, mental disorders, and co-occurring mental and substance abuse disorders...project total fiscal impacts under alternative implementation scenarios. In addition to fiscal outcomes, the institute shall estimate the long-run effects that an evidence-based strategy could have on statewide education, crime, child abuse and neglect, substance abuse, and economic outcomes..."

Developmental Disabilities (2008 Session)

Study "review of research on service and support programs for children and adults with developmental disabilities, excluding special education, and an economic analysis of net program costs and benefits. . ."

Crime, Criminal Justice Costs, & Prison Construction (2005 Session)

"...study the net short-run and long-run fiscal savings to state and local governments of implementing evidence-based treatment human service and corrections programs and policies, including prevention and intervention programs, sentencing alternatives, and the use of risk factors in sentencing. The institute shall use the results from its 2004 report on cost-beneficial prevention and early intervention programs and its work on effective adult corrections programs to project total fiscal impacts under alternative implementation scenarios. . ."

Evidence–Based Public Policy in Washington State: The Road from Studies to Policy Changes

Outcome of Legislative Interest	What Works?		Cost-Benefit?		Policy Change?	
	Systematic Review of Evidence?	Specific List or General Finding?	Program Level Cost-Benefit?	Portfolio Level Cost-Benefit?	Legislative action?	Executive action?
Crime	Yes	Specific	Yes	Yes	Yes	Yes
Child Abuse & Neglect	Yes	Specific	Yes	Yes	some	some
K–12 & Early Educ.	Yes, and Underway	Specific	Yes, and Underway	Underway	some	some
Substance Abuse	Yes	General	Yes	Yes	some	?
Mental Health	Yes	General	Yes	Yes	some	?
Developmental Disability	Underway	?	?	?	?	?

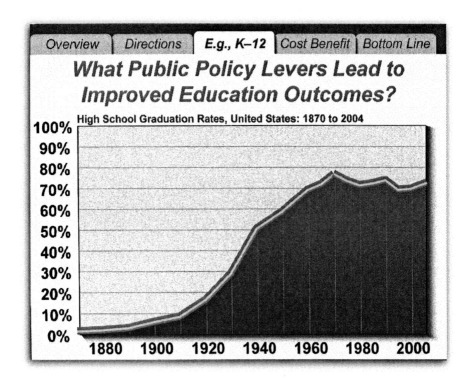

What Public Policy Levers Lead to Improved Education Outcomes?

High School Graduation Rates, United States: 1870 to 2004

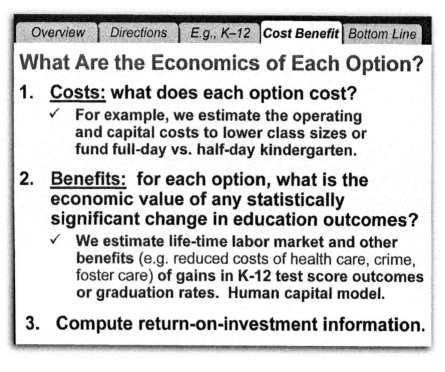

What Are the Economics of Each Option?

1. **Costs:** what does each option cost?
   - ✓ For example, we estimate the operating and capital costs to lower class sizes or fund full-day vs. half-day kindergarten.

2. **Benefits:** for each option, what is the economic value of any statistically significant change in education outcomes?
   - ✓ We estimate life-time labor market and other benefits (e.g. reduced costs of health care, crime, foster care) of gains in K-12 test score outcomes or graduation rates. Human capital model.

3. **Compute return-on-investment information.**

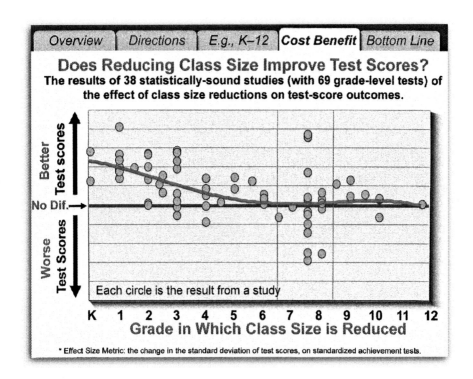

Does Reducing Class Size Improve Test Scores?
The results of 38 statistically-sound studies (with 69 grade-level tests) of the effect of class size reductions on test-score outcomes.

Better Test scores

No Dif.

Worse Test Scores

Each circle is the result from a study

K 1 2 3 4 5 6 7 8 9 10 11 12

Grade in Which Class Size is Reduced

* Effect Size Metric: the change in the standard deviation of test scores, on standardized achievement tests.

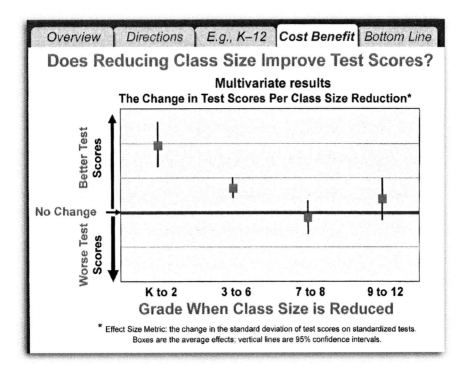

Does Reducing Class Size Improve Test Scores?

Multivariate results
The Change in Test Scores Per Class Size Reduction*

Better Test Scores

No Change

Worse Test Scores

K to 2   3 to 6   7 to 8   9 to 12

Grade When Class Size is Reduced

* Effect Size Metric: the change in the standard deviation of test scores on standardized tests.
Boxes are the average effects; vertical lines are 95% confidence intervals.

171

Cost-Benefit: Class Size Effects

1. ## Do Class Size Reductions Boost Test Scores?

   ✓ **The results are mixed, they vary by grade level:**
   - Yes, in K through grade 2.
   - Yes, (but less so) in grades 3 through 6.
   - Apparently not in middle and high school.
     (more research needed).

2. ## What are the economics?

   ✓ A one-unit drop in class size costs about **$220** per student per year (operating and amortized capital costs).

   ✓ For K-2, the return on investment (ROI) is **8.3%** (range 5.7 to 11%). This is equal to **$2.79** in benefits per dollar of cost.

   ✓ For grades 3 through 6, the ROI is **6%**.

   ✓ For middle and high school, return is negative.

3. ## Tentative Finding: Low-Income Students Benefit More from Reductions in Class Size.

Other K–12 Topics Being Analyzed as Part of Washington's K–12 Study

✓ **Factors in Current Salary Schedule**
- **Years of experience**
- **Graduate degrees**
- **Professional development**

✓ **National Board Certification**

✓ **Wage Levels on Recruitment and Retention**

✓ **Pay for Performance, Knowledge, Skills**

✓ **Extended Learning (school year length & intensity)**

✓ **Mentoring and Tutoring**

✓ **Teacher Aides**

✓ **English Language Learner Programs**

✓ **Others**

Appendix 3

The Pew Center on the States

☐ Advocates for nonpartisan, pragmatic state policy solutions to critical problems affecting Americans.

☐ Conducts rigorous research, brings together diverse perspectives, analyzes states' experiences to assess what works and what doesn't.

☐ Operates multi-state initiatives in sentencing and corrections, early education, elections , government performance and *Stateline.org*

www.pewcenteronthestates.org

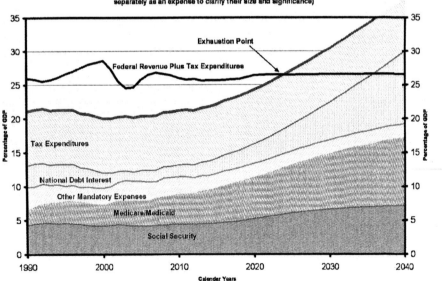

Total Mandatory Spending Will Exhaust All Federal Revenue Resources by 2024
(Note: Tax expenditures are added back to federal revenue and shown separately as an expense to clarify their size and significance)

States Face Long Term Spending Pressures

- Medicaid and Health Care
- K-12 Education
- Higher Education
- Demographic Changes
- Corrections
- Infrastructure
- Pensions and Post Retirement Benefits

A New Approach to Budgeting

- Increase the value placed on long-term interests

- Evaluate economic returns

- Subject all areas of the budget to comparable treatment in the budget process

- Regularly compare new and existing funding opportunities

Kansas: Recidivism a key driver

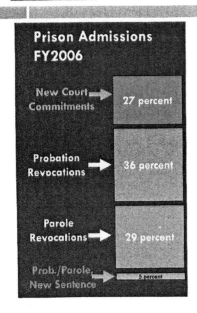

Prison Admissions FY2006

New Court Commitments → 27 percent

Probation Revocations → 36 percent

Parole Revocations → 29 percent

Prob./Parole New Sentence → 5 percent

65% of admissions

27% of the prison population

$53 million annual cost

Projected Kansas Prison Population
Fiscal Year 2007–2016

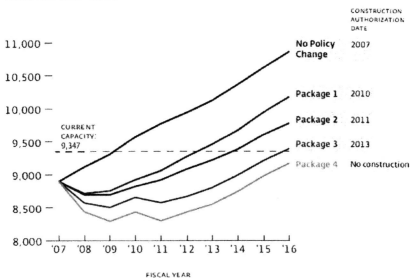

	CONSTRUCTION AUTHORIZATION DATE
No Policy Change	2007
Package 1	2010
Package 2	2011
Package 3	2013
Package 4	No construction

CURRENT CAPACITY: 9,347

FISCAL YEAR

Kansas State Grant Program

- Clear goal: reduce probation revocations by 20%
- $4.5 million in new funding
- Requires data-driven practices based on best practices to reduce revocations by targeting high risk offenders
- Continued funding contingent on performance

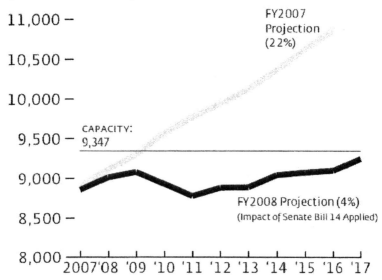

Kansas Projected Prison Population
(FY2007 & FY2008)

FY2007 Projection (22%)

CAPACITY: 9,347

FY2008 Projection (4%)
(Impact of Senate Bill 14 Applied)

Appendix 4

Estimating the Economic Benefits of a National Training Program

Art Berman
Twin Cities Rise!

Raymond Robertson[1]
Macalester College

Colin Hottman
Macalester College

September 15, 2009

Abstract: LaLonde (1995) and others have suggested that training programs that increase a worker's wages may add benefits that go beyond the individual worker to society at large. From a cost-benefit perspective, social (public) investment should not be greater than the total benefits (individual plus society). This paper provides an updated range of estimates of the potential social gains from a training program and illustrates how various assumptions affect these estimates.

---

[1] Corresponding author. Professor of Economics, Macalester College, 1600 Grand Ave. St. Paul, MN 55105, robertson@macalester.edu.

I. INTRODUCTION

The 2008 economic downturn and resulting stimulus debate have renewed attention on the efficacy of government spending. The current crisis provides the opportunity to think carefully about the most effective ways to allocate public funds. One widely-accepted criterion is whether the benefits are greater than the costs. Efficient public spending merits the term "investment" when the benefits from public spending exceed the costs. It is obvious, therefore, that effective spending decisions require accurate estimates of the costs and the benefits.

One attractive area for public spending is in worker training. Economists have firmly established a link between wages and productivity, between wages and education, and education and productivity. In an environment of high unemployment and falling wages, training programs become particularly attractive.

While the cost estimates of these training programs are often straightforward (the costs are simply the amount the program allocates per worker), estimating the benefits from training programs is more complicated for three main reasons.

First, there is much debate about the link between any given training program and the resulting change in a participant's wages. The main reason for this debate is that it is often difficult to perform a truly random experiment that would allow evaluators to determine what would have happened to workers in the absence of training. That is, at least one study (Feinstein, Galindo-Rueda, and Vignoles 2004) suggests that firms are able to pick the workers most likely to gain from training and, while these workers experience significant gains, workers not selected would not have experienced gains if they had received training. Thus, it is important that any publicly-funded program convincingly show that it is clearly adding value to the worker that would not have occurred otherwise. Techniques for evaluating a given program's effectiveness are part of a separate body of literature from the one this paper hopes to contribute to. Rather than evaluate whether or not any particular program is effective, this study addresses a very specific question: if a particular program is effective, what would the possible gains from such a program be?

Second, estimates of benefits generally depend heavily on assumptions. As is well known, it is relatively easy to selectively choose a set of assumptions in order to present a limited range of potential statistics in order to advocate for a particular point of view. Many different, and often opposing, assumptions may be equally valid. The goal of this piece is not advocacy. On the contrary, the point of this study is to highlight the range of assumptions that would affect the relevant estimates and, as a logical consequence, provide a range of estimates that could help inform the public debate.

Third, the required data for such estimates come from a wide range of sources. We address this problem directly by bringing together the latest data from numerous sources to provide estimates of the gains to both the individual and to society. The sources and methodology are explained in the sections that follow. In Section II we describe the theoretical foundations that guide our data collection and analysis. Section III contains the estimates and describes the effects of various assumptions in order to provide the relevant range. We offer conclusions and suggestions for future research in the final section.

II. Estimating the Economic Benefits of a National Training Program

The benefits of worker training accrue to three groups. Trained workers benefit from training to the extent that training leads to higher wages. Firms benefit from worker training to the extent that training increases worker productivity. To the extent that productivity and wages rise, society also benefits (Machin and Vignoles 2001). The gains to society have been estimated in a few notable economic studies (LaLonde 1995). Our goal is to estimate some of the gains to society that could accrue from a national training program and update some of the older estimates.

Gains to workers and firms justify their investment in training. Likewise, gains to society beyond the gains to workers and firms justify government investment in training. To generate initial estimates of the benefits to society of a national training program, we begin by following a study done by Barbara Ronningen and Tom Gillaspy in the Minnesota Demography Office (July 20, 1995). Our results indicate that the present discounted value of the gains to society over a ten-year period from a training program that moves one person from minimum wage to $12/hr ranges from $17,639 to $203,614.76. This range is across eight different sets of assumptions and all fifty states, excluding Washington D.C., for reasons explained below. To explain the range of estimates, we present several of the scenarios that we considered.

A. GAINS TO INDIVIDUALS

We first calculate the benefits to individuals moving from a full-time minimum wage job to a full-time job earning $12/hour. Because we consider a national training program, we apply the most recent available data for each state for state-specific variables (such as minimum wage and public assistance).

The Fair Labor Standards Act establishes minimum wage, overtime pay, recordkeeping, and youth employment standards affecting employees in the private sector and in Federal, State, and local governments. The minimum wage for covered nonexempt workers were increased to $7.25 per hour on July 24, 2009. Overtime pay at a rate not less than one and one-half times the regular rate of pay is required after 40 hours of work in a work week, but we do not consider overtime in this study. While the level post-training wages is arbitrary, a 2008 report by the JOBS NOW Coalition calculated that the minimum wage needed to cover basic needs for a single adult with no children was $12.05 per hour.[2] The same figure for a single-parent with one child (the scenario used in this study) is $18.07. As there are few training programs that would claim to be able to raise a worker's wages from minimum wage to over $18.00/hour, we use the more modest figure of $12.00, keeping in mind that this study, where possible, chooses to err on the side of moderation so as to get a better estimate of the lower range of the potential gains of training programs.

We include both federal and state taxes paid, as well as the change in Temporary Aid for Needy Families (TANF) benefits for workers with one dependent. The federal and state income taxes are constructed using 2008

---

[2] This calculation assumes 52 weeks at 40 hours per week each year.

federal and state income tax rates and the NBER Taxsim application.[3] These tax calculations assumed that workers were single, had one dependent, filed as head of household, had no income other than wage income, paid $400/month in rent, had no child care exemptions and received $600 (in unemployment benefits for the year) in addition to the state-level average total TANF benefits. Given these assumptions, the NBER Taxsim application calculates federal and state income tax liabilities. We use 2008 state-average TANF payments in our welfare calculations. Because the figure of $12/hour is constant across states, the variance in returns to individuals is a function of state-level welfare benefits and the difference in state-level minimum wage.

The range of gains to an individual under the assumption that workers lose welfare benefits (including unemployment) and have a higher tax burden[4] once they begin working at $12/hour range from $3883.77 in Alaska to $10,538.76 in Kentucky. The average across states is $7,834.45.[5] These results assume that all workers are trained because under a market-based incentive training program, training establishments are not paid for workers who are not placed in jobs. We did not include fringe benefits in these calculations. Therefore, these results should be considered an underestimate of the personal gains from training if workers move from jobs without benefits to jobs with benefits.

B. Benefits to Governments and Society

To calculate the benefits to State and Federal Government, we focus on eight scenarios. These scenarios are summarized in Table 1. We first calculate the gross gains to the government as the change in income taxes (state plus federal, again calculated according the assumptions above) plus the change in sales tax revenue. To calculate sales tax revenues, we assume that 30% of each additional dollar earned is spent on taxable items and therefore multiply 30% of the increase in income times the

---

[3] The Taxsim application is available at http://www.nber.org/~taxsim.
[4] Or, more accurately, receive a lower payment as a result of the EITC. The federal tax burden for minimum-wage workers is negative, meaning they receive money from the government. As wages rise, the amount they receive from the government falls.
[5] The value to individuals in Minnesota is $9,856.07. The JOBS NOW Coalition report cited above also notes that in 2007 32% of Minnesota jobs paid less than $12.05 per hour.

sales tax rate for each state.[6] We then considered the effects of the change in welfare benefits (moving from the state average to zero along with the reduction in unemployment benefits), the change in prison costs, and the effects of a spending multiplier. We discuss the method and estimates of each in turn. Without the change in welfare costs, prison costs, and the multiplier, the one-year range of benefits to the government is $1,925.25 (Washington) to $3,547.42 (Kentucky). One important characteristic of training, however, is that the gains accrue over time. Therefore, we calculate the 5 and 10-year present values of these benefits (using an interest rate of 2%). The 10-year values range from $17,639.59 to $26,179.12.

INCLUDING WELFARE GAINS

The 1996 Welfare Reform Law phases out benefits to individuals, but not to dependents. Therefore, moving workers to "living-wage" jobs may help states reduce welfare costs. I next calculated the gains to government under the assumption that states' payments of welfare go from the 2006 state-average to zero for trained workers. The high welfare-paying states (such as New York, Alaska, and Vermont) have the largest gains when people move off of welfare, and the low welfare paying states have the smallest gains. The one-year gains range from $4,317.98 to $11,950.73.

INCARCERATION COSTS

Figure 1 shows that violent crime and the unemployment rate move together through time. A similar pattern exists with total crime. Several academic studies[7] find evidence that crime and/or incarceration are positively related to inequality and unemployment. One study in particular[8] suggests that states may be using prisons as a substitute for social welfare programs. To the extent that employed people are less likely to commit crimes, states can save money in incarceration costs by investing in workers who would otherwise be at risk of committing crimes.

---

[6] Five states have no state sales tax: Alaska, Delaware, Montana, New Hampshire, and Oregon. We use values of zero for the changes in sales tax revenue for these states. Several states have exemptions for food and/or clothing that would reduce the share of income spent on taxable goods.
[7] For example, see Arvanites and Asher (1998).
[8] Beckett and Western (2001).

The most recent data for incarceration costs are for 2006. The Bureau of Justice Statistics provides data on the direct expenditure for correctional activities at the state level. These data are broken down into capital expenditures and other corrections activities. Capital expenditures include building new facilities and took up about 82.6% of overall corrections spending for fiscal year 2006. For each state, we take the total spending on corrections activities and divide them by the 2006 prison population, also provided by the Bureau of Justice Statistics.[9] This quotient provides our estimate of the average incarceration cost per inmate. Counting this measure as savings is only reasonable if the probability of going to jail without training is one, and zero with training. Since this is clearly not realistic, an estimate based on actual incarceration rates is more appropriate. Therefore, we consider the possible savings that could accrue to governments by assuming that training reduces an individual's risk of incarceration from 5% to zero (the average incarceration rate across states is 0.76%, compared to a rate of 4.6% for Black males)[10]. This implies that a given worker would have a 5% chance of imposing the cost of incarceration on the state. Therefore, when calculating the welfare gains from reducing the probability of incarceration, we add 5% of the per-inmate incarceration to the gains described above.

Adding incarceration costs to the increased tax revenue calculated in scenario 1 results in a range of 10-year gains to governments running from $22,670.98 to $40,371.61 with an average of $29,659.92.

These costs are likely to be underestimates of the true saving to society. In addition to lower incarceration costs, reducing crime also reduces the economic and psychic suffering of victims. The United States Department of Justice[11] estimates that victims lost $17.6 billion in 1992 with the mean loss for all crimes of $524 per victim. To the extent that training can reduce crime, it could reduce the losses to victims as well.

TAXES, WELFARE, AND PRISONS

The final scenario adds both welfare and incarceration cost savings to

---

[9] Technically, the prison population used in this study is the number of sentenced prisoners under the jurisdiction of State or Federal correctional authorities June 30,2005 to June 30, 2006 as listed in appendix table one of the report "Prison and Jail Inmates at Midyear 2006 NCJ 217675."

[10] Sabol and Couture (2007).

[11] Klaus (1994).

the increased tax revenue from the first scenario. The range for the one-year gains to states ranges from $4,480.09 to $12,217.08 with an average of $7,214.45. The range of ten-year gains ranges from $41,047.63 to $111,935.75 with an average of $66,100.52. Minnesota's one-year value of $6,800.86 per worker ranks 30th, with New York having the highest value and Tennessee having the lowest returns to the state.

ECONOMIC ACTIVITY MULTIPLIER

Another factor that may be considered as a benefit to training is the "multiplier" effect. When workers increase their income, they also increase spending. This spending, however, becomes income for others who, in turn, increase their spending, which becomes income, and so on. In the simplest Keynesian model, the multiplier is approximated using the marginal propensity to consume (which is the share of income that is spent rather than saved) and the marginal propensity to import. The marginal propensity to consume is positively related to the multiplier, since increasing spending increases the income of those receiving the spent money as income. On the other hand, the marginal propensity to import (which is the share of income that is spent on imports) is negatively related to the multiplier because money spent on imports does not become income for workers in this country.

Economists debate the importance of this effect and there is no firm consensus. Traditionally both the marginal propensity to consume and the marginal propensity to import have been high in the United States. A recent report by Romer and Bernstein (2009) uses an implied multiplier of 1.60.[12] The Minnesota report, however, assumes that the value of the multiplier is 1.55. We chose to use the lower estimate of 1.55, which implies that workers will spend just over 64% of the increase in their income on activities that would then lead to additional spending by those receiving the money from the newly-trained workers. In that sense, the effects of the multiplier come from the increase in income from the individuals and therefore we apply the multiplier to the individual gains. In order to

---

[12] Cogan et al. (2009) dispute this multiplier and suggest that, especially in longer-run scenarios, the government spending multiplier might be less than one and falls over time. Their estimate applies specifically to government spending under the argument that government spending crowds out private spending. When dealing with individuals, however, it seems more likely that this critique would not apply as the increased spending is the result from increases in productivity.

isolate the impact of the multiplier alone and avoid counting the gains to individuals twice, it is necessary to adjust the multiplier and use $mpc/(1-mpc)$ as the multiplier, in which the mpc represents the implied marginal propensity to consume. As noted above, a multiplier of 1.55 implies an mpc of 0.645. The resulting suggests that the increase in economic activity due to the increase in income would be equal to the gains to individual workers multiplied by approximately 0.416.

The resulting one-year gains in additional activity range from $1,616.55 in Alaska to $4,386 in Kentucky. Minnesota's value is $4,004.62, which is about 9.1% below the overall average of $4,386.58.

C. TRAINING CURRENTLY EMPLOYED WORKERS

Although firms and workers could both benefit from additional training, several academic papers[13] suggest that the nature of skills may lead to less training than would be optimal for society. Worker skills can be classified according to who benefits the most from these skills. *Specific* skills are those that are valuable to one (or few) specific firm. *General* or *portable* skills are most valuable to a large number of firms. Firms are likely to invest in specific skills because they enjoy the benefits. Firms are less likely to invest in portable skills because workers who receive these skills are more likely to leave the firm because another firm, which does not pay for portable skill training, can offer that worker higher wages and entice the worker away from the training firm.

Since firms do not have much incentive to invest in skills that are valuable to its competitors, the burden of paying for general skill training falls upon the workers. Workers, however, often face financial constraints. The national student loan program is one example of a program that recognizes these constraints and enables (future) workers to borrow the money they need to pay for training. The government supports this program because it is correcting a *market failure*. Without the backing of the government, students with little or no credit history are risky borrowers. A similar argument may suggest the government has a role in supporting training for existing workers.

---

[13] For example, see Stevens (1994) and Acemoglu (1997).

D. Some Important Considerations

In general, the gains to governments are greater than the gains to individuals. To the extent that the gains to individuals are negative in some cases, there is a clear role for government leadership in worker training. The government already does have several training programs in place now, and this analysis does not address the differences between the market-based approach and current programs. The economic literature that evaluates current training programs is contentious and therefore a more detailed comparison between the current programs and the market-based approach should be considered. Given some of the estimated returns to training, however, it seems clear that the current expenditure per trainee may be less than optimal and that, on a simple cost-benefit basis, more training would be beneficial.

It should also be noted that these gains might be understated because they do not take into account other forms of benefits. For example, the benefits of improving training may also extend to families. Children from higher-income families are often more likely to pursue more education. Training workers may therefore also benefit children and future generations.

III. A Case Study: Twin Cities Rise!

The numbers above provide some estimates of the possible returns to a national training program. Government and non-government training programs exist across the country. Government training programs (such as the Jobs Traning Partnership Act (JTPA) and subsequent programs) have received much attention in academic literature. Non-governmental programs, however, have received much less attention. To illustrate some of the possible returns to society from such programs, we provide an example from Minnesota.

Organization Overview

Twin Cities RISE! (TCR) is an anti-poverty non-profit organization based in Minneapolis that provides a work and life skills training program to people living in deep poverty over a 12-15 month period, culminating in placement in a full-time job paying on average $25,000/year with benefits.[14] TCR provides an instructive case study for this analysis, as its program and outcomes are well documented. TCR conducted its own cost-benefit analysis, which has been reviewed and tailored for the purposes of this report.

BASELINE FACTS AND CONSIDERATIONS

TCR serves a population in the Twin Cities that is typically very poor, unemployed, and has not had success in long-term employment relationships. To qualify for the program, individuals must satisfy all of these criteria:

- must have a high school diploma or General Equivalency Diploma (GED)
- must have earned less than $20,000 in the prior year
- must own less than $7,000 in assets
- must not currently be chemically dependent or have a sexual criminal conviction.

Participants are recruited into the program at local welfare offices, drug courts, halfway houses, correctional facilities, and in neighborhoods where there are people who might be suitable and would benefit from this program. The average age of participants in 2008 was 33. Not all participants reported earned income. For those who did report earned income, the average annual wage was $4,274. Participants also had an average of 3.2 barriers to long-term employment. These barriers include having English as a second language, being unemployed at program start, receiving public assistance within 6 months of entering the program, mental health or other serious health issues, learning disability, unemployed 12 months or longer, unstable or no child care arrangements, and history of physical or emotional abuse. In addition, approximately 65% had criminal convictions.

Nearly 52% of participants in 2008 were female. Participants were predominantly African American (60%), but also represented other

---

[14] Assuming workers work 40 hours per week and 52 weeks per year, an annual income of $25,000 is equivalent to $12.02 per hour.

groups Caucasian (19%), Multi-racial (5%), and other groups (16%, which includes Asian, African, Native American, and Latino). On average, participants read at the 9th grade level and were generally receiving some form of public assistance. Nearly 34% of participants received medical assistance for themselves and dependents. Just from the State of Minnesota alone, the average medical subsidy received for adults was $4,128, while dependents received, on average, $ 3,300. The 46% of participants who received some form of financial assistance from the State of Minnesota received an average of $4,988.

IMPACT OF TCR TRAINING PROGRAM

As noted by LaLonde (1995), training programs generally bear a burden of proof to show that their treatment uniquely contributed to the increased income (and therefore subsequent social benefits) of participants. TCR!'s burden is somewhat easier to meet because of the population it serves. The average starting salary (excluding benefits) for 2008 graduates was $24,792, representing an average increase in earnings of $20,415. Participants exhibit generally high retention rates, reaching 82% in the first year and 72% after two years. Subsidies from the State of Minnesota following graduation fall to zero, and through increased wages TCR estimates an increase in paid sales tax of $402 per person and $1,270 additional paid in state income tax.

STATE OF MINNESOTA INVESTMENT IN TCR: COSTS, BENEFITS AND RETURNS

The State of Minnesota is TCR's single largest funder, investing $527,000 (or 17% or TCR's overall funded amount) in 2008. The State has provided funding since 1997 to TCR, totaling $3.5 million in 2008 dollar terms.[15] To determine the value of this investment to the State, TCR! used a discounted cash flow analysis framework. The State's investments under the Pay for Performance contract were treated as cash outflows in year one.

---

[15] The current funding vehicle is a "Pay for Performance" contract. Under this approach, TCR only gets funded if it achieves certain pre-determined success measures, up to an annual capped amount. While this specific mechanism is not directly relevant to the outcomes described here, it is indicative of an innovative, performance-based public/private funding approach that appears to be effective.

Positive cash flows were recognized in two forms: (1) the value of incremental annual State taxes paid by successfully placed participants starting in year two, and (2) the value of annual State subsidies that the State would not have to pay starting in year two. Based on the retention rate data above, positive outcomes were reduced to reflect that some participants were no longer in position after years one and two. The analysis also assumed that the second-year retention rate was constant for additional years because TCR does not track participants beyond their second year of employment. Cash flows were measured over a 7-year period, which is used as a conservative estimate because the average remaining working life of our graduated participants is well beyond 20 years. For a discount rate, the study used the State of Minnesota's long-term cost of funds, estimated at December, 2008 to be 5.5%.

Since the State of Minnesota started supporting TCR in 1997, the cumulative value of the State's investment is $3.5 million (representing a net present value of $14.1 million). The gains measured above suggest that the State's return on its investment is 295%.

This analysis framework takes the perspective of the State of Minnesota as an "investor", and includes only those benefits that accrue to the State that could be reliably quantified. Benefits that accrue to other parties were not included. These include the significant changes in individuals' earnings levels and the related impacts on families, children and communities, as well as the impact to the Federal government in the form of reduced subsidy programs (e.g., food stamps) and higher federal income tax levels. Also, certain State benefits exist but could not reliably be quantified, so they were left out of the analysis. These include the reduced costs of incarceration and the reduced costs to the judicial system of this program that supports employment for a population characterized by a history of significant involvement in the criminal justice system. Although these savings may not be large, excluding them suggests that the returns to the program above are understated.

IV. CONCLUSIONS

The social benefit of worker training programs has been analyzed for some time. This paper provides recent updates of the potential gains from a training program that moves workers from minimum wage to

$12/hour employment. The results provided here illustrate the possible sensitivity to different assumptions but also show that the gains to society—defined as the returns to the individual, government, and economic activity—can be significant.

To illustrate this approach, the paper also includes a specific case study of a non-profits training organization in Minnesota. This non-profit is a good one to analyze because the population it serves is arguably less likely to exhibit the same kinds of wage gains obtained by graduates in the absence of the program. The results of that program suggest again that the potential gains from investing in worker training could be substantial.

REFERENCES

Acemoglu, Daron (1997) "Training and Innovation in an Imperfect Labour Market" *Review of Economic Studies* 64: 445-64.

Arvanites, Thomas M.; Asher, Martin A. (1998) "State and County Incarceration Rates: The Direct and Indirect Effects of Race and Inequality" *American Journal of Economics and Sociology* 57(2) (April): 207-21.

Beckett, Katherine; Western, Bruce (2001) "Governing Social Marginality: Welfare, Incarceration, and the Transformation of State Policy" *Punishment & Society* 3(1): 43-59.

Cogan, John F.; Cwik, Tobias; Taylor, John B.; Wieland, Volker (2009) "New Keynesian Versus Old Keynesian Government Spending Multipliers" NBER Working Paper 14782, National Bureau of Economic Research, March.

Feinstein, Leon; Galindo-Rueda, Fernando; Vignoles, Anna (2004) "The Labour Market Impact of Adult Education and Training: A Cohort Analysis" Centre for Economics of Education working paper, London School of Economics.

Klaus, Patsy (1994) "The Costs of Crime to Victims" Bureau of Justice Statistics Crime Data Brief NCJ-145865, February.

LaLonde , Robert (1995) "The Promise of Public Sector-Sponsored Training Programs" The Journal of Economic Perspectives, 9(2) (Spring, 1995), pp. 149-168

Machin, Stephen; Vignoles, Anna (2001) "The Economic Benefits of Training to the Individual, the Firm, and the Economy: The Key Issues" Center for Economics of Education working paper, London School of Economics.

Romer, Christine; Bernstein, Jared (2009) "The Job Impact of the Amerian Recovery and Reinvestment Plan", available at http://www.ampo.org/assets/library/184_obama.pdf.

Sabol, William; Couture, Heather (2007), "Prison Inmates at Midyear 2007" Bureau of Justice Statistics Report NCJ-221944

Stevens, Margaret (1994) "A Theoretical Model of On-the-Job Training with Imperfect Competition" Oxford Economic Papers 46: 537-62.

Figure 1:
A Schematic for Gains
from Training Program

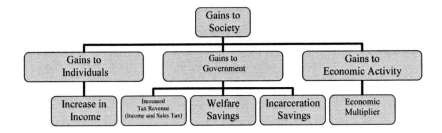

Figure 2: Unemployment and Violent Crime

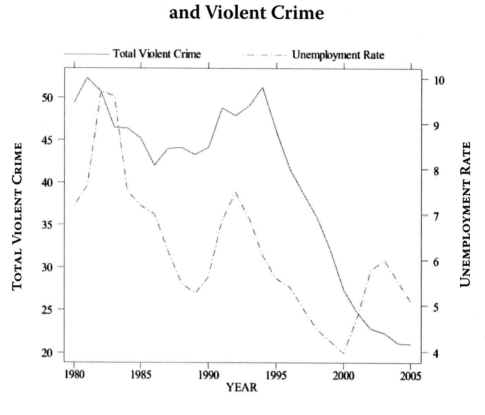

Notes: The unemployment rate is the national unemployment rate for individuals 16 years and older and come from the Bureau of Labor Statistics (www.bls.gov). The unemployment rate in the graph is the simple average of the monthly unemployment rate within each year. Violent crime data are the adjusted victimization rate per 1000 persons ages 12 and over and come from the Bureau of Justice Statistics from the U.S. Department of Justice (http://www.ojp.usdoj.gov/bjs/glance/viort.htm). The violent crimes included are rape, robbery, aggravated and simple assault, and homicide. The original data come from the National Crime Victimization Survey, whose redesign was implemented in 1993. As noted on the BJS website: "The data before 1993 are adjusted to make them comparable with data collected since the redesign. The adjustment methods are described in Criminal Victimization 1973-95. Estimates for 1993 and beyond are based on collection year while earlier estimates are based on data year. Due to changes in methodology, the 2006 National Crime

Victimization rates are not comparable to previous years and cannot be used for yearly trend comparisons. However, the overall patterns of victimization at the national level can be examined. For additional information about the methods used, see Criminal Victimization 2006.

Appendix 5

APPENDIX 5: MINNESOTA STATE AUDITOR'S STUDY
GOVERNMENT & PRIVATE CASH & NON-CASH RESOUCES AT VARIOUS EMPLOYMENT & WAGE LEVELS IN 2000*

Cash Resources	Not Working**	$6.00	$8.00	$10.00	$12.00	$16.00
Annual Earnings	$0	$12,480	$16,640	$20,800	$24,960	$33,280
USA. & MN. Taxes	0	0	-94	-318	-811	-2,031
Payroll Taxes	0	-955	-1,273	-1,591	-1,909	-2,344
EI Tax Credit	0	3,888	3,059	2,175	1,301	0
Working Family TC	0	972	1,330	1,055	633	0
Dependent Care Credit	0	0	103	138	251	0
Property Tax Refund	291	543	634	705	763	451
Child Care Expense	0	-60	-396	-576	-1,140	-3,600
MFIP/AFDC	6,384	0	0	0	0	0
Non-cash Resources						
MFIP Food Assist.	$3,084	$2,677	$98	$0	$0	0
WIC	363	363	363	363	363	0
Nat. School Lunch	404	404	404	326	326	0
Medical Assistance	5,952	5,952	5,952	0	0	0
Minnesota Care	0	0	0	4,716	3,876	2,616
Section 8 Housing	5,477	3,666	2,519	1,325	246	0
Energy Assistance	100	100	100	100	100	0
Total Resources	$22,055	$30,048	$29,439	$29,218	$28,958	$28,170
Annual Wages	$22,055	$12,480	$16,640	$20,800	$24,960	$33,280
Net Federal & State Support	$22,055	$17,568	$12,799	$ 8,418	$3,998	0

* Source: Office of the Legislative Auditor, State of Minnesota, "Economic Status of Welfare Recipients", January 2002. Benefits based on a family of three.

** Not shown above is the benefit for an individual working part time and averaging $5.15/hour. MFIP/AFDC applies at that wage so the net benefit is high at about $21,000.

About the Author

A Minneapolis native, Peter Heegaard began his business career in 1960 with the Trust Investment Group of Northwestern National Bank of Minneapolis, which he headed from 1980 to 1986. He was founder and former Managing Principal of Lowry Hill, an investment subsidiary of Wells Fargo. He retired March 31, 1996 to serve as consultant and community volunteer to several foundations and non-profit organizations..

In 1997 he founded Urban Adventure, a Twin Cities based educational program that has exposed nearly three-hundred leaders in business to our most challenging urban issues. His book *Heroes Among Us* was published by Nodin Press in September 2008. It covers the lives of eleven Minnesota social entrepreneurs who founded many of the leading regional non-profit organizations. In June of 2010 he was awarded the Degree of "Doctor of Humane Letters" from Augsburg College.

Heegaard is active in a wide range of civic organizations. He currently serves on the boards of the Philips Eye Institute, Ready 4 K, Northstar Foundation and One Percent Club. His past board service includes: Board of Pensions Presbyterian Church USA, The Minneapolis Foundation, Charles K. Blandin Foundation, Minnesota Council of Foundations, Minnesota Medical Foundation, Hennepin County Library, the Citizens League, Legal Rights Center, Presbyterian Homes Minnesota, and trustee of Macalester College.

Heegaard is a member of Plymouth Congregational Church and a former member of St. Luke Presbyterian Church where he served as Elder. He is a graduate of Dartmouth College and the Amos Tuck School of Business Administration. His favorite pastimes include fly fishing, hiking, cross country skiing and biking. Heegaard lives with his wife Anne in Minneapolis, Minnesota. They have three children and eight grandchildren.